BE STILL MY
Heart

Looking From the Inside Out

SUSAN F. GLENDENNING

BALBOA.PRESS
A DIVISION OF HAY HOUSE

Balboa Press books may be ordered through booksellers or by contacting:

Balboa Press
A Division of Hay House
1663 Liberty Drive
Bloomington, IN 47403
www.balboapress.com
844-682-1282

Because of the dynamic nature of the Internet, any web addresses or links contained in this book may have changed since publication and may no longer be valid. The views expressed in this work are solely those of the author and do not necessarily reflect the views of the publisher, and the publisher hereby disclaims any responsibility for them.

The author of this book does not dispense medical advice or prescribe the use of any technique as a form of treatment for physical, emotional, or medical problems without the advice of a physician, either directly or indirectly. The intent of the author is only to offer information of a general nature to help you in your quest for emotional and spiritual well-being. In the event you use any of the information in this book for yourself, which is your constitutional right, the author and the publisher assume no responsibility for your actions.

Print information available on the last page.

ISBN: 978-1-9822-6085-9 (sc)
ISBN: 978-1-9822-6084-2 (hc)
ISBN: 978-1-9822-6083-5 (e)

Library of Congress Control Number: 2020925664

Balboa Press rev. date: 02/16/2021

I dedicate this book with love to
All the spiritual seekers-become finders
In this world, who also love to love and to co-create
Miracles with their Beloved, Inner Being
As do I.

SUSAN FLORA GLENDENNING

CHAPTER ART

The following paintings and poems are from original works of Art created by the Author, Susan, and provide insights into the various chapters of "Be Still My Heart."

To order originals or color prints of these fine art, pastel paintings, please visit www.susanglendenning.com

CONTENTS

FOREWORD

By Doyle McKim,

"It's traditional that an autobiography is a true account of the writer's life. This work, *Be Still My Heart*, by Susan Glendenning, goes far beyond her life to a highly sensitive look at the growth of her soul. Here, she reaches deep into her heart to find the exact words that bring her spirit's reality to the surface for close study. Susan's disclosure of the incidents she has experienced, physically, mentally, and spiritually, makes it clear that she is a special being in all ways, as well as an accomplished writer."

By Doyle McKim, Writer, creative writing instructor, and editor

ACKNOWLEDGEMENTS

It is with much appreciation that I wish to acknowledge

*Helen Nenson, my dear friend who always encouraged me and shared the
Soul Journey of Love and creativity with me*

*Everyone mentioned in this book and also Doyle McKim & Marcia Jacyna
For their invaluable support and editing
Also to Connie Dudgeon French for early editing and encouragement
My loving family, Spiritual Guides, Big Brother
Jesus, A Course in Miracles, my*

*Spiritual Sisters, friends and teachers who model the principles
And relationships this book embodies*

*Esther Hicks whose loving dedication has taken her around
the world, teaching and living the principles of Well-Being
and alignment with her Inner Being, Abraham*

*Also to Mother Earth, our lovely planet, its plants and creatures
That also inspire me to poetry, music and art*

*And last but not least, for You, my Beloved Inner Being, for teaching me
To love unconditionally and for leading me to experience
These many Be Still My Heart moments.*

INTRODUCTION

By Susan Glendenning

I have loved feeling for, and finding, my *Spirit connection* since I was very young. I talked to *God* regularly. Visiting ministers taught my family the fundamentalist approach. They taught us to study the Bible to validate the specialness of Jesus, but said little about the natural revelations we too might embody if aligned with the love and miracles of our Elder Brother, Jesus.

Fundamentalist preaching baffled me. I could not understand their ideas of hell. Just how creating a place of fire and brimstone could ever be loving, or helpful, I could not fathom. Their problematic logic influenced me to look elsewhere for my answers. Instead of frightening an eight year old to join his way of thinking, the red faced, finger pointing man caused me to become very clear. I knew just what to do. I ran to my bedroom, threw myself on my knees and prayed. "Please God; *please* take care of that hell business!" My desire to know and understand God's Love and miracles of course, continued.

I loved the Old Testament poems of David, stories of miracles and acts of faith from people like Abraham, Moses, Daniel, Isaiah, Shadrack, Meshack, Abendigo and Job. These stories got me excited and led me to believe love and miracles must be available for all of God's children. I wanted to *live truth*, not to save the world, for surely God had already taken care of that. I wanted to prove *to myself* that miracles were still possible for everyone. Surely miracles could not be limited except by our beliefs and understanding. So, I continued to talk to my Spirit, and to trust this loving connection I could feel.

As I grew older, and opened myself to realms I could feel but not see, my family panicked. They challenged me, prayed for me and when all else failed, shunned me. I continued to look to my loving Spirit to help me find my way. The result is a blended love, mine and my Spirit's, a depth of encouragement and this book.

I believe everyone is gifted with sacred moments when our Souls' leave their signatures in our lives, moments when little bits of heaven illuminate our hearts. Even in our darkest times when we disallow Spirit and turn away, our Soul Force remains true and calls us to new ideas, benefits and opportunities, onward to ever new awareness born from our conflicts and dreams.

I began to hunger for spiritual wisdom at eleven. By twelve I remember praying for my life to somehow become helpful. At fourteen my whole world changed with one prayer, as you will soon see in Chapter one. Today I know we all add blessings every day and even, rather especially because of, our *mistakes*.

In the beginning I had no idea what form my gifts would take. In the mid nineteen eighties an encouraging friend practically demanded I write a book. After reading the Foreword I had written to a small handwritten book of Earth poems, she wanted to read the back stories, and asked for the events that led up to the many revelations, visions and healings I spoke of.

Her book request surprised and scared me. I felt how much I wanted it and at the same time did not have a clue how to make it happen. What fun I would have discovering in the next thirty-five years how to allow-it instead. I came to know my Spirit could and would help me accomplish all I needed. I never dreamed it would take so long, but then I have loved the process and wouldn't change any of it. Surely, I will always be led from delight to delight, from adventure to adventure in moments of continued awakening and love with my Beloved. I love my life and hope for many more years to come; but I am far too old to be silly or shy any longer. It is time to let my signs and wonders fly.

Now, I give you *Be Still My Heart,* my book whose stories, art, poetry and wisdom will hopefully transport you straight to the mountaintop of joy I have felt by modeling relationship with the Divine and providing memorable processes for your use to leap into the welcoming lap of your Source. Don't fear to engage a loving relationship with your Inner Being. Let your meditations, insights, sensations and hunches lead you to the processes and symbols you and your Spirit can work out. Go for it.

-With love, Susan

When Focus Begets

When focus begets love within you
And the journey to it becomes your thing
Then you will feel your non-physical Inner Being
And see its miracles in everything
For every choice promotes a perception
That will return to you in its kind
May happy thoughts become happy habits
Helpful seeds from your satisfied mind
Then love, fun and genius will chase you
Being so inspired by your happy deeds
This is the story of my choices
How these Soul Signatures came to be
© Susan Glendenning 2020

CHAPTER ONE

The Beginnings of Trust

LITTLE GIRL & THE MUSIC BAND
© Susan Glendenning Art & Poetry

*Let your appreciation and joy lead you deeper and deeper
into the boundless love of Spirit. You will return calm and
shining, quite naturally bringing back gifts for all.*

THE MISTAKE THAT CHANGED EVERYTHING

You are always loved and never alone.

Somewhere I heard the sentiment: "Our worst mistakes bring out our best gifts." I could only hope this was true because I tripped nearly every time I entered the pew at church. Awkward, skinny and flat chested summed it up. Too young to appreciate my finer qualities I took my woes to my mother who took them to my entire family! My Aunt Nell assured me my breasts would grow soon. Grandmother Flora showed me hers and assured me she never had any breasts before child bearing! Oh horrors. I failed to divert my eyes before seeing them hit her waist. Everyone meant well, but I needed help. Perhaps make-up…?

My parents talked about modesty and the dangers of fornication, but not so much about beauty of spirit. My southern bible-belt background intended well, but like other teens my consuming concern was to *be pretty*. Certainly no one, including my parents, would guess my agony from surface appearances. My life displayed a wonderful normality.

My younger brother, Steve, always made me laugh. My friends adored him, too. To see us all doubled-over gasping for breath was a normal occurrence at our house. Stevie's TV impersonations of Crazy Guggenheim and our youthful antics compensated for any adult stuffiness and our extreme mirth brought everyone great happiness.

I remember mountainous veins popping out on Daddy's forehead from arguing politics. Of course, Mother was much too proper to curse, but broke a hairbrush once, as it careened off the wall. Though sometimes strongly expressed, my family did not speak of personal feelings. By presenting oneself with a dignified reserve one might receive the benefit of acceptance, where as being silly might earn you a yell. In our house, serious things were most definitely serious. I remember scrunching down quietly in our car's back seat after Church. Steve and I listened for celestial music, beautiful slow tones that sounded on and on. No one else seemed to hear them so I squeezed back any word of my soul's passion for divine mystery. It seemed better to visit the passing clouds outside the window than to risk sharing the wonderful, nameless feelings of freedom and love that I felt welling inside me.

In the secret sanctuary of my bedroom I gave myself total liberty. There I never judged the release of my passions. Often I cried for the beauty of things. I remember sitting underneath the card table by my bed and weeping for the beauty and magnificence of *Tchaikovsky's First Concerto.* My bedroom provided a great refuge. There I created an artistic haven with art-covered walls and my precious piano with no ivory on its keys. This spiritual safe-place also protected me from nightmares such as memories of my first restaurant date and lap-full of flipped cantaloupe!

My parents fully met my physical needs as I grew, however my adolescence presented them with unforeseen challenges. We had this problem about make-up. My mother and I continually wrestled over appearances and ideas of beauty, especially eye makeup. Once mother scrubbed my eyes in the sink! Such brazenness was forbidden to me. How was I to know what a 'hussy' looked like? To my parents, beauty was easy and obvious. "Just be like Mama! She's beautiful!" Dad would say. So I spent time alone in my room. In my quiet sanctuary of creativity, I wrote, drew pictures, read Kahlil Gibran and talked to Spirit while smiling at myself in the mirror.

Outside my room however, our battle of wills raged on as these mysteries remained unexplored. But then how could my parents have known my first compliment from a boy arrived on the same day I tried mascara at a friend's house? I am sure they also never knew my clever art at twelve, circumventing their demands prohibiting leg shaving; I only shaved one side! I could appear wonderfully obedient by crossing the outward, more attractive side with friends, and the inner, horribly hairy side, when near my parents. They could not see my glorious blossoming from child to passionate young woman. My family tried hard to protect my image and my virginity with their parents' Old Order Brethren mores.

In those precious days I also experienced deep mystery and required no prerequisite of intellectual comprehension or cajoled agreement to find and feel my faith. I knew God lived inside me long before any understanding in words arose. I scored my Bible with coded colors and added poems and stickers that inspired me to the blank back pages. I prayed with all my heart and never doubted my family's teachings about miracles. I experienced piercing sweetness, as if joy and pain related. Sunsets, music and often the preacher's words opened an overflowing well of these sweet feelings.

By the age of fifteen I managed to possess equal portions of awkwardness and grace. Once, after being asked to pray the Sunday blessing at a friend's house, I looked up to discover all eyes staring at me. Their mouths fell open and eyes blinked in wonder. All I did was pray. Still the astonished table of guests sat frozen in their Sunday clothes, studying me. Perhaps they never heard anyone pray with gratitude? With chewing gum in one hand and the other over my heart I had prayed of my appreciation for each one. I thanked God for the lovely food and the kindness we shared. I named each person, "Thank you for Char and Al, Tommy, Allyson, Anita, David and their guests, and especially that You, Heavenly Father, love us all." Little did I know that same sincerity would soon open heaven's door.

Back home in my house, clouds of darkness gathered. After our yearlong battle over who would possess the make-up, neither side had progressed across the truce line. First Mother took the make-up from me, and then I sneaked into her bedroom, scouting through her vanity drawers until I found and confiscated it back from her. On and on it went. This challenge must have driven my parents mad. It certainly consumed their focus, for helpless to harness or control me, the struggle continued. This time, and rightly so, they nailed me. In their eyes I had committed a cardinal sin. I had broken their sacred rule of appearances. Acting on a not so brilliant idea to change the shape of my face, I thought to solve my perceived problem of ugliness. Witness my deed:

"If only I had a forehead." I surveyed, twisting a curl on either side of my face. Something clearly wasn't right about my forehead. There just did not seem to be enough of it. I also wished my eyes would slant up exotically and practiced twisting a lock of hair up tightly with a bobby pin to accomplish the look I envisioned. Being full of innocence and possibility, a brilliant idea struck me. Innate confidence bolstered me as I quickly secured my razor from the pink and black tiled bathroom we all shared. Secure once again in my room I peered into my vanity mirror, "A snip here and there might help, and anything would achieve better results than doing nothing!" So, I carefully lifted my bangs and shaved the hairline on either side of my forehead.

Then the death knell struck. Oh my, what had I done? What doom had I brought upon myself? Alas, unbridled youth and limited coiffing skills had rendered my appearance a real mess. Now what? Such a blatant act could not be hidden. Of course my mortified parents gasped and exploded in rage at the sight of me. As they rushed away I collapsed amidst the rubble of my broken self on the bed, shamed, shunned and broken-hearted. Alone and wilted in my silent room, the extreme pain of adolescent leprosy set-in and rendered me outcast from all I loved. Never had such humiliation descended upon me. Never had I felt my parents' love so withdrawn. I buried my face in my pillows and sobbed. I held my heart tight to avoid it cracking open. My life, my security, my place in my world, my parent's love, it all vanished.

The next day mother rushed me to a hairdresser whose jaw dropped at the very sight of me. First her eyes opened wide and then squinted narrowly. With wrinkled brow and chin tilted high she surveyed me. Then sinking her weight back onto one hip she quietly asked, "Whatever happened to your hair?" Avoiding the dread silence, I quickly answered ... "I had brain surgery!"

Back in my solitary room on that day of my worst mistake in life, I ached from crying painful tears. Cut off from my family's love, embarrassed and trapped in an error of my own doing, I turned inward, to the one thing I believed could transcend the events and stories of my life. I prayed to God, my Source, "Thank goodness, You still love me!" Somehow, despite my naivety I laid down my problems long enough to reach for a better feeling thought.

All of a sudden, exquisite gold and white sparkles of light rained down on me from the corner of my ceiling and filled me with more love than I had ever felt. Glorious white and golden light, unmeasurable love and its immense presence filled me. Finally I could take no more and asked it to stop. Obediently, the sweetness, the pain, and the light, all disappeared.

Yes, I had barely reached the ripe old age of fifteen, yet in one moment everything in my life changed. I remain profoundly astonished how by means of that one moment of innocent prayer, through one moment of allowing, belief and surrender with nothing to lose, my watchful Spirit was able to reach into my soul, gain access into my depths and lift every ounce of my precious being from belief into certainty and knowing. This attentive love would always hear me. I knew it, saw it, felt it. Of course, the instigating sadness evaporated. My heart only held room for overflowing wonder. From that day forward, with all my heart, I knew we would always be loved and could never, ever be alone.

Funny Hair at 15 with my future husband

Evolving coif at 16

COLLEGE COUNSEL

How I longed for someone to tell me about God,
who I was and how those two fit together.

T he dark, wooden floors of my Meredith College freshman dorm
creaked from our footsteps. Tall, cavernous halls, polished by
the lives of many girls touching the space, glistened in a mellow
mood. Certainly I had landed on another plane, one already hinting of my
rights of passage into self-discovery.

After saying goodbye to my parents it was time to unpack. Hoisting
my bag onto the twin bed, now pushed against the window wall, I traced
the memory of their smiling faces once more in my mind as I unpacked.
Like the setting sun outside my second floor window, echoes of their tender
voices faded all too soon into the warm autumn walls.

My mother told me that day was the first time she ever saw my
father cry. I would miss them during the mandatory, six week freshman
quarantine, but I was ready for the brave journey upon which I had
embarked. At least I thought I was ready.

Decorating my side of the dorm room was another matter. What fun.
I enjoyed playing house as I created my own little sacred space. Every girl
was allotted a desk and a bulletin board. My art and mementos quickly
filled my wall and established a homey, familiar feel I needed. As I paused
from my work to gaze outside I noticed I especially liked the outlook onto

the large green courtyard of ancient Oak and Ginkgo trees. High hedges and stately brick buildings surrounded me with a feeling of royalty.

But before details, before arranging anymore things, I dug for my treasure. Grasping the tall tube from my bag, I unrolled my large, poster-sized picture of Jesus and hung Him squarely over my bed. His smiling eyes warmed the little corner and protected my sleep space from so many foreign environs. The snickers by my door confused me. You see, I thought all people had their own authentic relationship with Big Brother. "After all, it was a Baptist college, wasn't it?"

My high school, creative writing teacher's love for Meredith first evoked my interest in the grand old school. I easily fell in love with its many charms. The fact it boasted a location only a few blocks from N.C. State did not hurt. No matter what evoked its charm, those first days challenged me on many levels. Despite the strange newness and uncertainty, I prayed with all my might for guidance. I prayed over everything: which classes, which teachers. Somehow I managed to get through.

My first day matriculating with each department took some effort. At each station the same challenge appeared. "Please write your last name first," the teachers and aides would ask. Tired as I was, from the ordeal of dealing with so many people, they droned on, "You don't understand, please write your *last* name first." Of course they never heard of a last name like Flora, they merely observed yet another mixed-up freshman. It always took several times telling, before they understood I had written my name correctly.

Still, I had much to learn about my new world. The assignments constantly pushed me beyond my limits. Never lacking interest in learning, I enjoyed most of it, but puzzled at the breakneck speed we seemed bound to travel. I missed an understanding of our destination, and missed the sweetness of relating as we relocated again and again into yet another class.

My religion professors in this all women's Baptist College in Raleigh, NC, called "The Angel Farm", seemed intent to challenge us to think anew, to compare, memorize and find errors in dogma I had never questioned. My favorite hymn, *In the Garden*, was ridiculed for bringing God down to our level. The very idea Jesus might now walk and talk with anyone, whether in a garden or not, seemed to be outrageous to them. I could feel my Spirit had my back and helped me feel love whenever I asked. Though not spoken in words, it seemed God was being taught as outside, distant and far beyond anything we might comprehend or access.

Particular philosophical approaches to God had not occurred to me. I had not needed any. I wondered, "How else except in application would we learn anything?" Existentialist concepts of a meaningless life presented me with a large puzzle piece, not in my picture. It would be thirty years before I dared comprehend the meaning behind such an idea. All I understood told me my personal relationship with Spirit determined my reason to be. The simple hymn represented Love's embrace of me, ours of God and Its of us, regardless of our unwitting errors. I found it difficult to connect with the ideas my professors offered.

I left the ivy covered walls to search out someone who did know and talk about God. I decided to visit a church! Freshmen were not allowed cars in those days, but in light of my clear decision I became bold. I'd take a bus. The simple act of finding a bus, for the first time in my life, filled me with excitement. I commanded the world. The Sunday sun smiled on my journey as I climbed the sunlit steps into the enormous white Methodist church. The awesome structure ascended into sparkling light over my head and promoted its ideas of power and glory. I slid into a back pew and awaited my help; surely here, I would find relief.

The preacher's words flowed with passion. I know, because I clung hungrily onto each one. The hour passed and still I waited. No word of God rang clear. The lively minister spoke only of the evils of alcohol. His words left me cold and built no bridge as he demonized the poor suckers who might try to live outside his important rules. Utterly dismayed, I left the church and vowed to make an appointment with the head of the religion department.

The next morning I invited the wisdom of my religion professor. "Please, tell me what you know about God?" I implored. "Would you share your faith with me?" But instead of answering, he adjusted his wire-rimmed glasses and asked me what 'I' thought. Suddenly the lovely book filled room became stuffy. When he began a discussion of ethics, about right and wrong, all the air seemed to leave the room. Even he, an important college figure, spoke not a word of a personal relationship. Untangling my skirt from the chair, I excused myself and summoned what precious little energy remained to head for the door. Spiritual matters I took seriously. Nothing now remained for me, but to withdraw into seclusion.

I found an isolated storage area on the upper floor of my dorm occupied only by large boxes and suitcases. I squeezed myself into a small corner where the ceiling angled low. Comforted by the darkness and alone at last to cry, I let my tears fall. Day turned into night as I waited, unsure how to deal with my dilemma. I found nothing familiar in this strange new world. Adrift among the baggage and unable to comprehend, I sat alone with my thoughts. No one seemed to care or know anything about God. Did all these people think Bible stories were just stories? Did they not understand there was something very real here? Had they not found Spirit's hand real? Did they not build their lives on knowing these things?

As evening enveloped me my answer came. Points of light, which I interpreted to be the Apostles, punctuated my night and spoke to me in a vision. A broad universe of stars opened before me and filled me with understanding in bursts of whole thoughts, rather than individual words. They comforted me and encouraged me to go back; all would be fine. Their kind message told me mere words could not contain or fully communicate Spirit because words were symbols and never meant to substitute for the meanings we might discover in our experiences of the Divine. We can turn away but never be lost from God's love. My guides chose the best words available for their time and understanding, the same as we do now. Our acceptance of God's love allows for experiences that bring knowledge. I was not to fear; no one could invalidate my experience. I heeded their counsel to be patient with myself and my world. Upon finishing my second year, I changed my major from religion to art, and began to focus my joy in creativity.

How I had wanted someone to tell me about God, who I was and how those two fit together. The universe answered and spoke to me, not because '*I*' was special but because I trusted and waited for my help. The heavenly counsel, "not to worry" met me where I stood in a way I could comprehend and use. The experience validated my trust in my own spirit guides and afforded me the freedom not to have to measure my experience with other men's tools.

I have found that each moment, no matter how bleak, can be turned over on inward-ground. Our inward focus on God's love engages our awareness of that love within us. It is there we will learn of the love we are that dissolves problems.

GRANDFATHER FLORA

♦♦♦♦♦

Until the Twelfth of Never I'll Still Be Loving You
Lyrics by Paul Francis Webster, Music by Jerry Livingston

Nearly ten years had passed since college. So many years since I heard Spirit in my head saying, "I ask not that you be something you are not, only that you be all that you are." I married my childhood sweetheart, moved to Germany for four years, then on to Alabama and now to Olympia, Washington with our two little girls. Rooms full of unpacked boxes punctuated our new home as news of my father's massive heart attack stunned us. The timing could not have been worse. We had just transferred to a new state three thousand miles away from family. My normal resilience began to drain away as I stood alone and empty handed in the boxes. A swoon of withering homesickness pursued me across the 3,000 mile divide and shrouded my heart with heaviness. Extended travel with two small babies was out of the question. My eyes filled with tears.

Then suddenly, as if tapping me on the shoulder, my deceased Grandfather Flora's presence filled the room. The music of our song lilted from the radio and surrounded me with the warmth of his love. My memory flew back to my adolescent bedroom where I had sung to him. He sat beside me on the creaky piano bench in my artsy, teenager bedroom. Unaffected by my floor to ceiling art covered walls, bulletin boards full of fashions, awards hung on my closet doors, make-do collection of furniture or my worn and tinny old piano with no ivory on its keys, my grandfather remained focused on me and received every note I sang. Again my love for him overflowed. The words and melody of our song played to my senses and flooded my heart with his compassion. His spirit was singing my song back to me. I felt him returning the promise, *"Until the Twelfth of Never, I'll Still Be Loving You."* The thought of his kind, black eyes watching over me from heaven, nearly stopped my heart.

I felt his presence comforting me many times over the next months and years. Gradually the dramatic shivers of recognition faded as I focused on other things. I accepted his visits as natural and began to function from a peaceful heart again. I never really believed in an endless sleep of death; certainly access to his boundless love had not been limited. My dear father in North Carolina recovered and life smiled again for us all.

I think back with wonder about my childhood and the depths of love grandfather and I carved out for each other while sipping iced tea and smiling in silence on the front porch glider. What grace to step outside the everyday rush and task-filled world, to settle into the moment and accept peace together? I believe the unconditional delight we found in each other's presence emerged from our joint permission to be just that: who, what and where we were, together.

Now our continued connection in love, like a light in the dark, dissolves the world's boundaries and joins us on a new level. The unexpected warmth and sweetness of his loving presence in combination with the familiar song still speak to my understanding of just what is real and how meaningless the power we give death.

LURA FLORA

Remembering my grandmother four years later

My grandmother, Lura Flora, understood the lusty side effects of playing in paradise and never scolded me for blackberry stained teeth or for having too much fun. I always felt good being near her. On vacation in her welcoming presence, my childhood easily flowed into young adolescence. The very idea she allowed my brother, cousins and I to mash the ice cream bananas with our hands, way offset any deficiencies being short, plain or old might pose. I paid little attention to her appearance, though I remember she wore no makeup. Color was far too worldly for her. She even contained her permed curls with a homely hair net.

Closing my eyes to remember, it is her great warmth I cherish best. She dared touch me and hug me, kneading my knees like a cat whenever I sat near her. Guiding me by the arm into the big kitchen chair, she asked all the right questions as she sweetly listened and looked into my eyes. Rapt attention is heady stuff at any age, and most likely the reason my brother, Steve, and I always agreed to performing the many solos she asked of us whenever we visited.

Though busy motherhood and thousands of miles lay between us, nothing could bar the interplay of our deep connection. I learned unconditional love from my grandmother. Now the passing years signaled it was my turn to pass on, and to extend the kindness I had learned at her knee.

Though my days overflowed with life's abundance and blessings surrounded me, my grateful heart yearned for service and for my life to become a blessing. So I prayed for God to use me, even my mistakes, like the times when I failed to be or know my best. Surely Spirit might find a way? Shortly after praying this I began having some unusual psychic experiences. After several occurrences I willingly cooperated with the process.

> Without warning while sitting at the piano, engrossed in the middle of my playing, my whole body would suddenly go limp. I nearly collapsed over the keys. Confused yet affected by this unnatural event, nothing remained but to aim for the bed. I argued all the way up the stairs, "I don't believe in sickness. I am not sick. I don't need this," Then I would fall on my bed. While lying there, exhausted and drained, not yet understanding, I began automatically praying, "God help me understand this."

Stretching out my arms and legs felt good as if an invisible windmill spun love out through me into the universe. A wordless realization would then tell me, of course, "Someone needs your loving prayers!"

The energy tickled my hands and feet, as it flowed out to whoever needed it. Allowing love to flow through my body beacon, I continued to extend love. Soon either an image of a face or a feeling about someone in particular, usually one of my *Meals on Wheels* customers would pop into my mind.

Then by my fondness for them and the strange signal, my *Meals on Wheels* partner and I visited to find them usually in the hospital. I sang, held their hands and extended love in the same way I had received from Grandmother. They usually died within a day or so. Like an angel at the gate, I accepted my sweet role of loving and never questioned. Stories of this got to be a joke with our *Meals on Wheels Coordinator*, Ida Jane Taylor, who laughingly implored me, "If ever I get sick, and you visit me, please... don't sing!"

But this time at the piano, as I wilted over the keys, I did not argue and marched willingly straight to my bed. Bolting upright I knew it was Grandmother! Clutching my heart, I began to gasp, cry, and scream "Nooooo!" in my mind.

Just then, awareness of her swept over me. She was not alone! Granddaddy had joined her. Ten years or more had passed since he died and now he greeted Grandmother! I did not see their physical bodies. Rather I felt their essence as their energy swirled a dance of loving all around me. Surely stars streamed from their twirling path! Sharing their joyful union put any fear and sadness to rest. They were fine and judging from the excitement I could feel, they were better than okay. Love goes on and on, blessing and growing, and always increases.

A very short time passed and the phone rang. It was my mother. Before she could phrase the news, I answered, "I know."

CHAPTER TWO

New Perspectives

BIRDS IN PARADISE
© Susan Glendenning Art & Poetry

Upside Down

I've been searching for something
All my life
Something bright and something true
I've given my body, served and trodden
Searching for love outside of me
In you
Upside down it seems
This fair reflection of my dreams
I've looked everywhere
But within me
Here

UNCONDITIONAL LOVE AND A DRAWER FULL OF SPIRIT TREASURE

*Time for bravery as I accepted partnership
with something I could not see.*

Stockings were hung by the flickering fire. Christmas Eve's artichokes and hors'deuvres had been eaten on the good dishes under the tree by candle light. My husband, Tommy, our two daughters and I lounged and laughed on the floor in the glow of crackling wood and readied ourselves for the cookies and hot chocolate to come. How could it get any better? Our daughters put away the puzzles they'd worked with dad and made way for the grand finale: opening one gift before bed and Santa. Love and affection so saturated our living room I never wanted that night to end but fate and my husband's military requirements had other priorities. In the morning we would drive him to the airport to leave for two years Army duty in Korea.

We all functioned quite well on the way to the airport. It wasn't until we returned to the car without Tommy that I felt the full impact of his departure. I had to get us home. That's what I began telling myself as I stumbled against the cold gray airport parking wall. My heart was breaking and the car door weighed a ton. Yet here, getting into the car, were the two dearest little girls on earth. They depended on me. How could I hold myself together when I felt like sobbing? How would I drive? What kind of parent would I be without my light heart? How would I function when the man I lived for had just vanished before my eyes? Yet there were those two precious daughters sitting so sweetly in the back seat.

Thrust prematurely into a transformation I could not have foreseen, I folded myself into the front seat and began to drive our precious cargo home. Shaking and unsure, I turned inward to beg, "Please God, please help me get us home!"

I did not yet understand the power of my thoughts or my freedom to affect change with them. I perceived all problems to be coming from someone or something else, outside of me. But that was about to change because I needed help. I needed prayer's unconditional, connecting power and the possibility for depth and strength like never before. In the next single-parent, pioneering years I would have to seek answers and find strengths only sourced within.

Days and months passed when I asked myself, "What might lie within, just behind or underneath the see it, touch it, taste it world of my limited thoughts and acceptance? What more would I learn of the compelling love I felt?"

One evening as I lay in bed watching TV a breeze ruffled the curtains behind my head, just as the narrator on television spoke of Elisabeth Kubler Ross and her studies on Near Death Experiences. Sudden terror leapt like a ghostly surprise into my open mind. Something deep inside me stirred. In an instant the whole right side of my bedroom fell away into timeless, formless space. My sense of reality shifted. Literally gripping the bed and my old thought constructs at once, I bravely gathered courage to continue my search for truth in these new thoughts. What else might exist if not simply what I saw and accepted each day as reality? I wondered. Trying to focus on the narrator's words but failing, my mind continued asking… "How might I learn without endangering myself?" I dared look on. Of course I feared everything, because just then nothing at all was clear. So I counselled myself, "Random emotions do not mean doom is impending." Perhaps I did have something to do with the picture called my life? I noticed how, at times, I was able to leap far over potentially devastating hurdles, while at others when faced with much less challenge, I sank into my depths.

Despite my lack of intellectual understanding, each time I attempted to replace my negative thoughts with loving ones, I felt peace. Loneliness no longer tore at my heart. My inner work of observing my feelings kept me fresh, honest and generally positive. Each time I prayed, comfort followed. At times my mind would intercept and capture a beautiful truth. I wrote each one as accurately as possible on whatever piece of scrap paper I could find.

One spring day I discovered myself fretting so intensely that I blocked the sweet bird song outside my window. I couldn't stop worrying about our troubled world. Fights, shootings, prejudice and hunger appeared everywhere on the news. I decided to take this matter to the loving Spirit I called Jesus, or Big Brother. I asked for help to understand and this vision unfolded:

> I stood before Jesus on smooth white stairs. I appeared shorter and younger than he as I looked up at him from the step below. We both wore long white robes and the stairs appeared to float in a cloud. I carried a huge globe of the earth in my arms. As I held it out towards him, it erupted and oozed pocks of smoke and gunfire. It seethed troubles and problems of all kinds.

Searching His eyes with mine, my young heart pleaded for help and answers. His face of immense peace and softness, smiled as He gently took the ball from my arms. As I watched expectantly, he began circling his hand over it. As He did this, it began to glow with energy. Soon a rainbow of light encircled it!

His smiling eyes assured me there was no threat. In fact it was beautiful! No need to fear, for in the same way He would be with me.

Then I saw a joyous multitude dancing hand in hand also encircling the earth, celebrating and blessing us with love.

There in our Nisqually home, in my young motherly world, I received help I could understand whenever I stilled myself to listen. Over and over my answered prayers allowed me to trust and engage in the moments of my life as they were. I began to write what I heard as I prayed, reflected or allowed myself to capture while flowing through.

Once as I readied to leave for church I heard the sweet words begin to flow. I expressed my concern as I did have the children's choir to lead, but plopped down on the side of my bed to write. "You will have to take care of the time," I reminded spirit, and began writing the beautiful thoughts. Then touching earth once more with my awareness I noticed that after all that time writing nearly a full page, the clock hands had not moved one bit! This was the day I learned we could *go out of time.*

The little pieces of spirit treasure continued to accrue as I stashed them in my underwear drawer until one day *I knew* I must write them down properly. My heart pounded with excitement, unable to ignore the commission. The message to write spoke clearly. Indeed, I felt the message so strongly I knew my life as I understood it, would be over once the writing was completed.

Every cell in my body thrilled as I dared begin. The quiet hush in the house exaggerated every sound. The children slept blissfully while the kitchen table, cleared of all but all my snippets of paper attended the stroke of my pen. Bravely, I began to write the ponderous words of love. Suddenly I sensed an other-worldliness and realized I was not alone. I became aware of the scene as if from a higher vantage and watched myself write.

Winds tore around the house making eerie, wailing noises. The chimes on the deck swung wildly, clamoring their notes against the house. Daring to turn only slightly, I peeked over my shoulder to see the trees just beyond the porch stood absolutely still! Shivering from the powerful unknown I had entered, I wondered, "Could some force or resistant aspect of myself still terrified of change, be trying to scare me from my task?" Impassioned with resolve to write what I had learned in a form I could share, I squeezed my eyes and lips tight and shouted a mental "NO!" into the ethers. I would not stop! I would not give way to fear. I would write. I would bravely accept partnership with something I could not see and began to record the spirit treasure I had heard.

Such a feeling of victory and freedom welled up in me, I overflowed with soul certainty. Without a doubt, I walked my right path. Beaming an emphatic "Yes!" to my spirit, a current of recounted words soon filled pages.

Here following are some of the snippets I wrote:

> May you live to know the blessing your life is and share some measure of that love with the God who created you, and with your fellow travelers who also seek to live and dream and grow.

> When your life becomes too complicated, look back to the simple truths and gain strength and sight to look again at its mysteries.

> There is no real sin, only your denial of God's reality in your life. Through prayer, energy of God's will and telepathy of minds and hearts will come.

> This is how My love can be all around you, how it can fill you this very instant. Even if it sears your heart like a fire, swim in it. It is the dawn of a new day!

> May you know that Love ever enfolds you in its warmth, kisses you, rocks you and sings to you of the treasure you are.

> Oh little ones, be not swallowed up by cares and pleasures, not puffed up with hypocrisy and games. Humble yourself before your God, that you may live for love's service.

Parents, love is not born of obligation, but of love itself. Give it first and receive it. Demand it and lose track of it. To know it demands that you share it!

The idea to slow my mind when meditating and let go of all other thoughts came after I committed to go beyond seeking to finding my Source each day. I was about to wash my hair and took off my slippers so

I would not slip when these words rang in my ears: "The loves of your world are for your warmth, a blessing, but put them off when you come before Me to pray, for the loves of the world cloud your sight, oh ye who would see."

Trade in your realities for light. Trade them for God's realities and be strong. Be filled. Be drawn along by the inner stream and see the outer actions unfold perfectly. Soon enough God will give you eyes to see the destination. Worry not that God's time is a variable you know not. God provides for all.

I believe in you and pray soon you will find happiness, not in settling for less, but in believing in more.

Look beyond the window dressings of talent, interests and gifts. Strive to love the inner man: the real gift is the self that lies within.

Let not your hearts accept ill! Negatives waste space and blind you to God's light. Be careful to pray for everything, seeking guidance and wisdom for every day.

Be watchful little ones, gifts oft come in disguised packages. Missing my husband who still lived in Korea on military duty I cried, "Oh Lord, do not leave me also!" And the voice said, The aching inside you is from a heart too filled. Give love away and the pain will subside. Give and live, give and live, give and live! So I began to hug my *Meals on Wheels* customers and look in their eyes when I served them their meals, and my heart soared.

In the midst of my strivings I was tossed and torn, "I give you peace." Jesus said in my mind. But I cried, "Oh, my Lord, where, oh where is it?" And He said, "It lies within you, you have but to seek it."

With a twinkle in his eye he said, "Follow me." and I felt the strength of His steady arm. "Fear not, I have overcome the world." His eyes gaily smiled, as we crossed the treacherous mountain made of all my unfinished dishes and chores. Joy sprang once more in my trusting heart for I knew all my work would get done. With such a companion there by my side, I knew He would even help me enjoy it!

When you seek to serve only yourselves you find nothing, not because He gives you not, but because you perceive not! If ye demand to be filled... how shall ye be filled? Ye be filled already ... with demands.

Help thy sister and help thyself. But how will ye do it? Force her to some action? Be done with her quick? Obligate thy duty? Oh, as sparkling willow branches sway in love, walk in peace, *care* and with a heart full of helping, Love shall be thy fill!

I started a beautiful little journal. My simple life with the children provided a perfect backdrop for my clarifying focus with Spirit. I also remembered writing these words in the back of my Bible at seventeen. I heard them as I had walked and prayed one sunny autumn afternoon through the quiet forest near our house. Now in my thirties they called for deeper review as they made their way into my journal: "I ask not that you be something you are not, only that you 'be' all you are."

Fervent in my prayer for love I journaled to Jesus: Teach me without drastic means. I am willing. I am open. Because I am so limited by my perception, I pray for your help, that through love and perspective I might move beyond my limits! I've lost sight of the way to you and the happiness you give when I serve many times. But I pray this time, your mark be so firmly placed in my mind that I shall never be empty of love and joy again. Somehow, I believe it is true; this heart that burns with your love will never empty and never die.

IN THE GARDEN

+ ✦ ✦ ✦ ✦ +

I hear the call of Eden. I am answering in every choice I make for love.

My hunger for wisdom led me to many great teachers. I wept reading passages from Lincoln, Emmet Fox, Mary Baker Eddy, Unity leader Charles Filmore, priest Mathew Fox, and teacher Joseph Campbell. My mother cautioned me of the dangers of reading the devil's work, which surely would be present in anything but Biblical text. But I had no fear and trusted God to steer me clear of any such negativity as devils. I opted to seek freely and trusted my intuition to inform me of any resonance, danger or imminent growth I might need to know about.

My first experience of channeled wisdom came from someone called Ramtha. Channeling in its purest form occurs when one aligns their heart and thoughts with appreciation and wisdom while they open to the inner realms of their soul. One may then translate words and concepts from blocks of thought received. Bits of wisdom and esoteric information about the nature of consciousness may be received from ancient spirits, elders, angels, or our Beloved Source and Inner Being. Biblical prophets in days of old spoke to their communities with authority in this way.

On a film shown at Evergreen College in Olympia, WA I heard Ramtha speak through J.Z. Knight. He said, "One cannot achieve mastery until one has spent seven days alone with Mother Nature." The concept intrigued me. All my life I had enjoyed the outdoors but paid little attention to my relationship with it. To engage in a life to life dialogue with Mother Nature would necessitate all sorts of rethinking on my part. But this challenge was just the sort that interested me. So I prayed to my Inner Being, my Beloved, and set off.

> Beloved Spirit, I open my heart to accept the rushing, tumbling freedom of your love in this place, in this moment. Open my eyes to the beauty all around me. Feed my spirit with the milk of connectedness and belonging. For I would open my soul to the sacred wilderness around me and be filled with freshness, even know my kinship with all life.

Deliberately, as if on assignment, I opened to the experience of Mother Nature. My decision to know myself in this way opened me to new worlds of beauty. As I slowed my life pace and spent dedicated time discovering, I began to receive poetry. When I let my thoughts of appreciation flow unimpeded what I noticed…rhymed. Here are a few:

The Embrace

One day across a field of green
A wonder I chanced upon
A tall and twisting leaf of green
A delicate dancing fern

The quiet grace of wind and lace
Hushed all the forest 'round
As on and on its green lines danced
The gentlest show in town

Far down the gentle pathway
Through the forest green
I stepped so very lightly
As if inside a dream

With outstretched arms I sought to embrace
The sights and smells so fair
For a longing deep within my soul
Urged me know it and love it there

"It's easy," said the flower
"Tis nothing hard to do
Just open your eyes and allow your heart
To know the glory of all that's you"

Wonderful new energy invigorated me. Subtle beauty in the simplest
things caught my eye. The movement of a blade of grass rippled sensations
of joy inside me. Bird song tickled my ears. Rain drops rang-out like
orchestral bells as they splashed on bouncing leaves. The smell of wild
chamomile forced me to pause, and struck me to my core with delight.
The sky became a vast painting hung before me, as inside my pounding
heart recorded it all.

Dancing in the Morning's Glow

How the green does beckon me
Out into the glory of the earth so free
Round and round this day I go
Dancing in the morning's glow

Full with hopes and dreams for all
To know our divinity and answer the call
Sing me earth. Sing me dew
Fill my cup oh Daisy do!

Laugh me round oh magic sky
Till out among your clouds I fly
Misty air still soft from night
Cleanse my heart with heaven's light

Nature's parts working in harmony taught me of my inner self. As I listened for the song in each leaf or place I became aware of my own. Flowers and trees shared messages. Dancing ferns and raindrops symbolized greetings received and concerts of consciousness I could comprehend. Rhymes fired in my head whenever I hiked in deliberate reverence and appreciation. With senses fully alive, I stepped out as if for the first time, into a world where I felt God alive in me and in every living thing.

Rain Song

Pitter-patter, pitter-patter
bounce, plop, dash
Wondrous drops of water on a
fat leaf splash
Emerald light deepens in the
forest hall
While gentle rain teases
playing rhythms
on its soul
Pitter-patter, pitter-patter
bounce a crystal drip
The playful dancing splashes sing
I was born for this

Becoming bolder, I dared speak to ants. One bright morning the sun called me to the top of a little hill by our campsite at the San Juan County Campground. The children played and painted watercolor paintings with feathers; luckily I had forgotten the brushes. I found a perfect spot with a little dip in it where I could recline as if in a chair and spread my blanket beside sun speckled madrona leaves. In no time, pure bliss filled me. The cool, clean air crested over the rocky bluff and scented the air with ocean perfume. Out in the distance, gulls called to the breeching orca whales and wave diamonds sparkled, "Hello!"

As I began to write, I noticed ten or more ants crawling over my blanket. I decided to honor them by not killing them. I asked with my mind, in return they not bite me. Then, accepting my own proposal, I returned to my writing in the sun speckled shade. Suddenly I noticed *lots* of ants crawling over my bare legs and feet! To my utter amazement they did not bite! The strange demonstration of inter-species trust further fueled my journey, as I fell even deeper in love with life.

What a Wonder the Wildness

Who has seen a Madrona tree
Branching low
And dappling the ground

Where the spots of sun she let through
Meet and mingle
With mosses of down

Where the rocks cropped with lichen
Gray silver green
Laugh for the joy of the play

Tis heaven to sit and warm in her glow
In the wild
Where dried grasses be

'Neath warm and smooth arms
Golden red, fiery orange
Crunch her offering of fallen leaves

Fallen wherever they like, they may
They are free
To be lovely you see

I'm off to the wilderness, off to see
What a wonder
This wildness be

Appreciating the beauty of nature around me represented a dessert first kind of thinking that was easy and led me into an even deeper trust, with my Spirit. I learned how good it felt to open to all people and creatures as kin and began to grow wings of experience and faith that could carry me through any perceived difficulty.

Awaken my memories of you, Beloved Spirit," I prayed. "Renew my strength with your messages. Wash my soul with moonlight glow until all I see is beauty. I choose your joy. I hear the call of Eden. I am willing. I am answering in every choice I make for love.

BLISS AND STEW

*Like symbols in a dream or summer breezes across my table, life
is always matching me up with the tone of my thoughts.*

Loneliness stalked me as my bored fingers traced the brown, corded edge of my husband's empty leather chair. The children attended school and deprived me of their laughter's diversionary rescue. A trip to Korea was not likely so romance was certainly out of the question. Nothing seemed quite fair as I entertained negative thoughts like "My youthful prime might be wasting away."

As soon as I noticed the discomfort my negative attitude was generating, I decided to shake off my lackful thinking. I drew in a deep relaxing breath and listened for my Spirit. The word, *choice*, crossed my inner sky. Yes, I could toss routine to the wind and choose something different. I would give myself up to adventure.

Bounding outside and off my front porch like Super Woman, I learned the glorious sunny day had already begun to wipe away all dreary negativity. Morning clouds melted into turquoise and my body, now mimicking the sun's warmth, radiated cheery smiles. Several of my friends had taken *Inner Child* classes to free up their hidden innocence. Mine, never having been captured, gleefully ran the show. "A lunch date with myself, why yes!" my inner child proclaimed. This solo idea did not faze her in the least.

I could see no awkward shyness would impede this solo date. So off I floated into my favorite Korean restaurant, alone, abreast a sea of my own mirth and good will. My full-body radiance attracted smiles from every face as I made my way to a delightful table by an open door. Memories of past family gatherings flocked to mind: birthday parties, passages celebrated and general mischief shocking friends and kids as we ate little smoked fishes with their heads still on. Momentum continued to build as memories of other restaurants, some from Germany years before, joined my sunny perception. Invisible friends, these happy thoughts, crowded my table.

Today the owners of this small family run restaurant left the side door open, welcoming the breezes and pleasing my soul. Ivy twined its way around an indoor latticed screen. The birds' songs and sweet, leafy-green fragrance from the big tree outside, wafted across my table. Sitting there bathed in bliss, I wondered, "Why had I not done this before when such a simple act elicited so much sweetness?" I marveled at myself and found my degree of appreciation astonishing and still building. How quickly the combination of bliss and stew compelled a poetic response. Words flowed from my pen as naturally as the sky blushed to pink. With electrified pen, I described my joy-spiced stew.

Kimchee Stew

Hot, spicy stew, you warm the very pit of my being
How magical, a date with a bowl of soup
Enchanted by your bubbly welcome
I surrender my heart to you

There's love for the peppers and colors
love for the aroma that excites my soul
What a contrast, the hot and mild aspects
yin and yang even here in my bowl

Perhaps the secret to truly enjoying life
is to accept miracles in Kimchee Stew
Behold, I have found mastery
accepting wonder even here in my soup

Many times now, I've found simple miracles
by stepping aside from thoughts of lack or doubt
I'm no longer waiting, resentfully asking
"Well, where is it?" in grievous shouts

Now I choose to release the worry and doubting
and to follow the path of my heart
To delight in what I find before me
that's what choosing is all about

Perhaps Kimchee and Tofu aren't your favorites
Maybe you'll choose a different restaurant
Perhaps a walk, a talk or a picnic
something delightful your heart really wants

Accept your perception of what's before you
as a symbol of what you already asked for and got
Allow any obstacles to become mere mysteries
in process of revealing their secrets -- that's a lot

Love can then flow through any situation
and be sufficient for every need
Then we'll realize, perhaps we need nothing
For all will be miracles, indeed

Peace and happiness settled over me and the room. Like symbols in a dream or summer breezes across your table, life will teach us about our thoughts. Perhaps it is our way of looking at events that needs changing. Joy, patience and understanding will emerge if we look at whatever lies before us as something we already asked for and got.

Don't fear listening to yourself. Get up and open a window. Follow your heart.

HARMONIC CONVERGENCE

The world and all its problems faded from my view
as I perched on the end of our sailboat.

My husband returned mid service, from Korea and took us out onto the Puget Sound sea in our large boat. A miracle of creative financing had allowed our purchase of this forty-two foot sailboat and my husband and I seized every opportunity to discard routines and sail away in our new home away from home. We named her *Wind Song* and headed out at the racing speed of two knots. When I dared inquire about our speed my husband reminded me, at least we sailed faster at two knots than a wagon train heading west.

Sailing through the air with outstretched arms I claimed my watery kingdom. As soon as I felt my toes tuck under the bowsprit's smooth metal supports I sensed the transformation occurring. Right there in front of my husband and two daughters I transformed from wife and mother into some kind of mermaid royalty. In utter glee I owned it all.

"Never mind the tummy tickles," I told myself as I peered down into the dark and thrilling depths. The shimmering sparkles of sea spray marked our steady passage through the cold Puget waters and I liked the way the cool water tickled my hot skin. How exhilarating! This fine summer day begged me for adventure so I leaned into it. I felt beautiful being decorated with the ocean's sparkles of water and light. I felt the full-out spirit of summer herself flourishing inside me. So what if our massive forty two foot ketch shrank into a dot in the big deep water of Puget Sound... fun called me.

The lusty scent of freshly oiled teak welcomed me as I floated down the narrow stairs into the main cabin. Making lunch had called me from my bowsprit perch. Daily tasks presented new challenges in this unfamiliar rock and tilt world; walking and cooking became games to be enjoyed. I learned to pay close attention when making soup; one speeding motor-boat could roll my entire kitchen sideways. What kind of fun-house had we boarded?

How easily I returned to my childhood on this boat. Innocence, illusive and fickle on land, opened her arms to us here on the deep, and gathered us into her nurturing safety as we allowed ourselves to play. The world and all its problems faded from view as we splashed and romped over the deep green sea. Worries of any kind simply drifted away as I gave myself over to my royal adventure. In fact, hum-drum thoughts of any kind appeared particularly insignificant from the vantage of my hammock tied between the two masts.

I had scarcely seen my friends all summer; but on this particular August night, I would learn how connected we really were, distance or no.

Every nook and cranny of our sailboat served a dual purpose as we anchored this happy evening in the softly rippling waves and made our beds for the night. The table, once lowered into its proper position and topped with foam, changed from table to a magic carpet for our precious children. After tucking them into their beds I made my fun-house trek across the tilting floor to our starlit, forward V-berth. The cramped space required a bit of contorting but the adventure of it all more than sufficed. I climbed up into the cool night air, nestled into our big sleeping bag and gazed up through the open window into the lovely night sky. Fresh sea air kissed my cheeks, and sent me sailing on rock-a-by waves of pleasure. "Goodnight?" How could I ever close my eyes on such beauty, or on such a fragrant and briny sea? I fought my fatigue but soon lost track of days and time, as the starlight, sea smells and fresh air rained down through the open hatch onto my face. Finally I closed my eyes and whispered my surrender: "Thank you," whereupon I commenced a full night of lucid dreaming.

> I found myself observing a small, richly paneled Renaissance room. A monk worked steadily, decorating a manuscript illumination of the letters IHS. He wore a long brown robe, tied at the waist with a length of simple cording. Mechanically, he scribed the inky letters until a splash of golden sunlight burst through the open window of the small room and fell on his writing hand. He paused in surprise and appreciated the beauty. Soon other senses activated. He noticed the sun-warmed wood, the fresh air and the wash of rainbow colors rimming the windowpane's edge, all as if for the first time. Spilled into the moment with him, my mind spanned the ages of wisdom I had lived and the miracles I had experienced. I heard myself thinking, "What a profound book of experiences I could write now!"

> As if perfectly logical, the scene switched again, and I looked down on my body, as if from space. The shape was transparent and defined only by a thin blue outline of light. Inside this form I could see darting rays of light bouncing off the blue boundary walls, always moving. I asked my invisible, but very much present guide, "Why must the light be confined?'" Then the cells forming the boundary walls responded by spacing themselves; openings appeared between each cell. How exhilarating to feel the darting rays of light extending far. What ecstasy. My thoughts with my accommodating guide had freed them and best of all, I felt it. The cells opened. I had to think it first and then hold it, but I could feel the life force being freed.

> As if this adventure were not enough, I realized my guide encouraged me to question further. Freedom, inherent in

this vision state, allowed me to know anything. I could know whatever I wanted to understand quickly and absolutely. Anything was possible. So, I wondered, "How would I feel as a man, physically?" My childlike question did not disturb my guide as I instantly transformed into a man! My sexual anatomy felt natural. No distraction or discomfort interrupted my movements. Exultant with knowledge, I realized the learning tool I had been shown. "Knowing anything comes simply by holding the thought." In doing so, I became the answer to my own question. It was necessary to stay focused, of course, like a gymnast walking a high beam, but balancing in mind was not impossible, hardly difficult now! We could be and experience anything we could know with our minds. Was not each day manifest in the same way by our repeating habits of thought? The possibility of conscious thought and all its applications sent me spinning right back into my body.

No matter how insignificant and narrow my thought or point of view, no matter how happy or sad, conscious or unconscious, by holding a thought in my mind I would come to experience knowing it.

I opened my eyes, after what felt like a brief period of time to discover the entire night had passed and a new day dawning. Amazing! How refreshed I felt, and without sleeping? But I needed to write. A sense of urgency compelled me to begin before my memory of the night's deep mystery vaporized back into the vision realm! I scrambled through my bag and grabbed my checkbook. "Thank goodness for paper." I thought as I sat there in utter amazement in our warm and cozy sleeping bag and scribed my night's recollections.

How primitive our self-imposed limitations seemed in that lingering moment of sacred residue, how unlimited our choices. Our large boat rocked gently in the cool quiet of my waking world. Claps of wavelets cheered as my husband rolled over. I remained motionless and still only half formed, as I sat wrapped in the folds of my sleeping bag's warmth. "Our potential as Spiritual Beings has only just begun," I marveled. I recorded my amazing experiences and imagined sharing all this with my friends as I tucked the precious scraps of paper into my bag.

Now, back home, barely a week elapsed since our amazing sail and my lucid dream when I heard about the *Harmonic Convergence*. A concerted global endeavor, focused on helping the human race move into awareness of peace through the power of thought, meditation and prayer. Spiritual leaders hoped by sheer force of numbers to shift the balance of humankind's collective thinking out of fear, war and ignorance, into knowledge of Love. Prayers simultaneously rang out, sounded into the oneness by people of all faiths, from all nations. Magnified as if through a large crystal, a critical mass of conscious prayer aimed to magnify Love and then sweep back into the collective mind.

I crumbled to hear about the Harmonic Convergence. How could I have missed such an important event? Had I missed adding my prayers to the whole? But wait, I hesitated, taking in a deep breath. Tingles of excitement rippled through me. Had that night of visions and lucid dreaming been the same date? Had my simple prayer of gratitude engaged some switch in my soul and opened me into the energy of the cosmos? Had one small thank you been enough to activate the deep desire and intention of my soul? I checked the date, Yes! The dates matched: August 16th, 1987. Many other doors may have opened to the positive influence of this convergence. East Germany literally opened her doors and tore down the Berlin Wall.

How miraculous life becomes when we live in a state of appreciation. I had landed exactly where I needed to awaken to new insights. Everything had occurred perfectly. The playful change of scene from land to water had helped me disengage from my routine, yet something more worked that night's exquisite synchronicity. What had my guide taught me? What had my night of experiences shown me? Relax Susan. "Be there again. To know and feel a thought, one must allow oneself to be it, contemplate it and think about it without contradiction." That felt close. Oh, and hold it. "Practice the steady part. You need not chase experiences because it's all good. You can choose new thoughts that will attract new answers. Everything is possible and success tailored to each moment if you live in the high energy of praise and appreciation."

Now home again, I allowed my gaze to wander the beauty of all I saw. I noticed the steam rising from my morning coffee, and savored the snug feeling of sitting cross-legged in my chair by the window. I noticed chickadee wings fluttering at my swinging birdfeeder. Songbirds flit about and call to their friends, "Come enjoy fresh seeds." Outside dainty snowflakes bedecked the backyard trees. Fresh winter air danced in through the crack I opened in the window and white light filled the house as I appreciated it all. What beauty!

How does it get better than this? I asked. Then looking directly at me, a massive blue jay swoops in with a nod and dines. My soaring heart records it all and radiates another beacon: "Thank you Universe. Please, send more of this!"

CHAPTER THREE
Trading Realities

CONVERSATIONS
© Susan Glendenning Art & Poetry

The Voice Of Eden

I hear the *Voice of Eden* calling in my ear. It speaks of
Love unending, my time of choice is here.
I choose the joy, the joy of Eden.
No longer can I serve my fears again.
Oh Life that's full so full of beauty, I give your
Voice my ear. You're calling me.
Come home the voice is calling,
Eden's here Pilgrim, just see.
The choice is Love unending, knowing
Life is one with thee.
I hear the call, the call of Eden. No longer
Can I serve my fears again.
My Spirit soars, bursting with freedom.
I'm answering your call to come back
To the Eden that's
My home.

SPEAK TO ME

I am open… flow through me, I prayed.

O utside, red maple leaves flirted with the sky and danced in the wind as I read another book about someone's experience as a channel. The wise and masterful words striped away my defenses as suddenly as the autumn winds shook the trees outside my window. Like the changing autumn leaves, I longed to bridge the chasm of separation between myself and deep wisdom.

Suddenly a brilliant idea sparked in my mind: I would simply make it happen and busily prepared my assault on this uncharted realm. I had heard that Buddha simply sat under a Bodhi Tree until he received enlightenment. Why of course, I thought, as I resolved to do the same! There were no Bodhi trees in my living room that crisp, autumn morning, but determination and my desire to learn, strengthened my resolve. If not as a channel, I did have calligraphy talent. Perhaps automatic writing would help?

I collected a notebook and pen, sat down on the couch by the open window and closed my eyes. Though I prayed often, I had not conceptualized deliberate, mind-emptying meditation. I had done it… however not yet consciously connected the many flashes of wisdom I had received as being the result of slowing my mind. Too much quiet, the kind that might spin one's mind around, seemed a bit scary.

Yes, my whirling and chaotic mind energy felt strange, but I clung stubbornly to my intent and resolved to achieve some kind of deliberate contact. Could I be less than some other person? Why should I be left out, I challenged. Love and spiritual knowledge had long been my unerring focus.

My honest reasoning helped me agree with myself and calmed me. Just let go of resistance, Susan! Every muscle stilled in agreement. I simply would not get up. Someone would have to talk with me... and now!

After a few minutes of these dramatic thoughts, a deeper quiet fell all around me. The torrent of tumbled thoughts vanished. I sat hearing nothing and merely observed the silence. Still I waited; still the silence. The only sound I heard was my own breathing.

Small, but persistent, sitting there alone on a couch in the wide universe, I waited. At this point someone else might have given up, and never tried again. But I really wanted this experience. Stubborn by nature, I persisted. Something inside me knew the fairness of the universe shone no more or less on any other. One person could not be loved more than another! Like a baby calf rooting for its mother's teat, I stayed with my request, my demand. My over-confident self-will felt right, even necessary to fuel such a large leap into great love.

I decided to move my writing pen in circles like I made during calligraphy warm ups. Surely some supportive force would then move my hand with automatic writing. As I moved the pen in circles over the lines on the empty page, to my surprise, instead of automatic writing, I heard words in my mind! The Voice said:

> "Greetings Beloved, you are loved far more by others than
> you love yourself."

Immense power and love accompanied the words. In amazement I dropped my pen and let go of any attempt at automatic writing and melted into the communication.

48

"I have come that you and all people might be lifted up."

I understood perfectly what was being spoken. Yet, it heralded a meaning so much deeper than words alone could convey. Our identity, essence, spirit body, and power to love and create were so vast and beautiful, so divine, so majestic and serene. How could words contain the reality I sensed? Yet the voice continued. There was a reference to great joy at my willingness to open and interact in this way. I asked questions that were gently answered, and then moved aside for the greater answers, which I did not consciously know I had asked.

Later, I tried to capture the essence of what I had heard and wrote these words in my journal.

> "Higher than angels, unto the heights do you climb, to find that your Kingdom ever awaits you in perfection.
>
> "Unlimited joy as yet untapped in your life is yours as you let go living in the shadows of night. Allow others their lives, and begin to unveil your own.
>
> "Allow each moment to unfold you, to your Self. Everything supports your growth, even the issues that you fear the most. Time cannot hold you.
>
> "Hands reach across dimensions to comfort you, yet no one comes to freedom except by their own steps. Reconnect. The choice is yours. It is dawn and the light barely illumines your world. Yet the hopes, dreams and beauty can be seen. Have faith. More is coming.
>
> "Believe in the goodness of God. Believe in your ability to know and hear that voice for God inside you. Choose love in every instance and grow strong. Shine your healing warmth on all you meet. For like an arrow from God's heart are we sent to one another, sure, swift, and on purpose.

"Allow yourself more than an acceptable amount of love. Allow an open heart full, for you are loved so greatly. Let yourself feel this great wellspring of joy that is your birthright, and then live your life so in touch, so full and receptive to Love's spirit, you become pure in your expression of it."

Childlike determination and willingness held fast, aligned me with the energy of higher mind, and empowered my clear goal to open a door always inside. The kind thoughts in my mind voiced an irresistible, universal love intended for all. Still I questioned, "Why do we settle for so little in our day to day lives when mountain top experiences such as this feel so natural? Perhaps on that inward ground, where all are equal and connected, we will find the key to who we all are. There we may all find empowerment, communion, devotion and the celebration of God's love to be our common delight."

I prayed for God to teach me without drastic means. I was a willing learner and eager to embrace the inner, soul-searching work that any growth or responsibility-taking might involve. "Flow through me," my fingers strummed as my voice and guitar merged in prayer. "I am open… flow through me." I prayed and miracles began to occur almost daily.

GENTLY RISING

Look into your heart and reconnect with its wonder.
Watch the lotus open. Behold the thrill of fulfillment
never lost, but awaiting only your gentle return.

Mutual benefit, enthusiasm, and love's resulting light, must flow freely from an opening soul.

My spirit is like a breeze, gently rising and swelling
I float and linger with joy and thanksgiving
Even like a fragrance upon the ether
So swells my heart

I saw myself not unlike an eagle, flying high
Over the earth with peace and thanksgiving
Filling all the spaces of my heart

I called out, "But where is my path, Great Spirit?"
And I was caused to know it was here in this moment
And it was unlimited and safe

Then my heart sprang for joy and like a song
I whispered through the air

Turning I descended and asked,
"How will I show them how magnificent You are?
How will I show them this view?"

Spirit answered me, "Not save they fly.
Then you can lead them to this spot.
They will see if they faint not."

"But what of finding them," I asked?

"Are you not all brothers and sisters? I was answered.
Is not the light shining in you as a lamp that cannot be hid?
Dispel darkness with joy.
Find new heights in thanksgiving.
Be blest evermore my child, my song."

Taste true freedom. Relax and open into the flow of infinite love. Pause wherever you are and come to rest in the safe arms of your Spirit.

THE VOICE OF EDEN

I felt myself fly out over the top of the sound,
as if I were riding on a wave.

My daughter sat at the piano and embellished runs and chords of music that I felt must have transpired from a higher calling. Her sweet nine year old frame spoke volumes of power as she disregarded my chaffing to practice, and insisted on making up her own thing.

Music made me weep, swoon and travel inward. I felt it. At nine I also had begun my musical journey. I bought an old upright piano with money from two savings bonds I had saved. It looked as if it had come from an old saloon and mattered little that no ivory graced its keys, for I was in heaven to have it.

My first teacher was humble indeed. She shared the hymn, *Almost Persuaded*, as my first assignment. Needless to say, I was on my own. My father, was very proud of my musical interest and allowed me to write the names of the notes directly onto the worn, wooden keys. He also encouraged me to teach him whatever I learned for the first little while, then gratefully receded, patient to wait for the day we might sing together. Warmed by his smiles, and impassioned by the sounds, I promised myself to play for God. Little did I then dream how the gift of music would stir me.

My family moved from Georgia to Mississippi when I was in the fifth grade. My new music teacher tried her best for one and one half years to teach me something. The nearly impossible task frustrated her as well as me. I felt great passion associated with the sounds, but had no patience for theory. Too distracted by her constant, "Un-uhs" which punctuated my every error, I dreamed of going home to play the piano on my own. To put it simply, she wanted theory and I wanted *Malaguena*!

Eventually, she decided I was ready to join her skilled group of students for a recital. We picked a perfect Sonatina. The runs and regularly patterned notes in the left hand accompaniment enabled me to really get into it, without thinking. When I could *feel* the melody, the notes came out right.

Eventually the frightful moment of performance arrived. The students sat at attention in polite rows, with hands crossed mannerly in their laps. The auditorium filled as area piano teachers and their students gathered for an impressive affair.

The smart-looking little group of children all dressed to the nines, quickly disappeared from my thoughts as I wrestled with the practical difficulty of merely sitting on the bench. The hoop under my dress of ruffled net stuck straight out. I could barely move or be seen under the fluff of stiff layers. My stockings were also especially shocking, the way they matted down my unshaven legs! Finally forgetting my trappings, I let go into the simple notes.

A flood of unexpected power raced through my eleven year old body and lifted me off the piano bench as I ended my song in a thunderous <u>Ta Dum</u>, *not written in the score!* Glancing up, I saw the row of teachers a gasp. My piano teacher sat bolt straight, eyes wide, in what I perceived as disapproval.

Tremendously happy to be moving out of state again, I left her scholarly care for the wild freedoms of North Carolina. Happy never to receive, or ask for further lessons, I left the realm of left brain campaigns, content to cultivate my own style of music.

Now, all these years later, I had a daughter with talent and I certainly did not want her to repeat my mistakes. I sent her to the very best teachers. I was glad to hear they used keyboards and could turn off the sound occasionally I wanted them to insure her knowledge of theory and not allow her to play so heavily reliant as I, by ear. I felt I had fulfilled my duty. Yet still, Jennifer did not want to learn. I even recorded her masterful compositions. I felt certain she must have reincarnated some master's talent! Finally I realized it was *me* who wanted to play and compose music.

Waiting until the house emptied of all possible witnesses, I sat down at the piano. Barely breathing from excitement I dared place my hands on the beloved keys. I pushed through my hesitation and began to play. Voila! I could create lovely melodies too! My notes flowed as Jennifer's had and excited my deepest heart.

My budding spirit, giddy as a sprite, danced for joy as I encountered this new realm of possibility. The idea of trigger melodies that might awaken soul-connections played in my mind. I hungered to bring down gifts of music and prayed before each session. I listened each day for notes to write. So what if I heard only three notes. I would not stop. I would not let go of my dream. I knew the demonstration would be so miraculous, not even I would doubt its origin. I prayed:

> I would know my life as your music, for I am your instrument, tuned and reverent in your hands. Play me. Sing through me. Express the passion of my soul, great author of my intention, my Beloved.

Quite a scattering of eighth notes filled my papers before I realized they comprised a song and the strange chords contained the accompaniment! Then one day in the shower, I became the melody I was singing. The beauty of the notes and the commingling of ideas and feelings flowed through me nearly erasing my single body identification. A love and gratitude for what I perceived to be nature's majesty combined with my intention to move forward into the uncharted reaches of my heart and exhilarated me. The words and melody I sang also sang me. At some point I realized if I were quick, I might capture it on tape. Racing through the cool air, dripping notes and water, I captured fragments of what became my first of many, fully notated songs, *The Voice of Eden.*

Once I sang for a funeral and felt myself fly out over the top of the sound as if I were riding on it. I remained aware of my fingers strumming the guitar and of my voice continuing to sing the song *Tis a gift to be simple, a gift to be free,* but watched it all from the vantage of sitting on my own shoulder. Afterwards, the hush in the room broke into tears of praise and remembrance. One person told me they had never heard anything so beautiful. I knew it was Spirit that we had witnessed in our moment of joining, in our moment when the veils between the worlds thinned.

For years my dear soul sister, Helen Nenson and I worked on a musical creation called *Transcendence.* The joy of co-creating never ends. Since her passing my every moment's thought of it feels miraculous. Her belief that we could do anything gifted us both. Enjoy your dreams, the wilder the better. Then life sparkles for you.

CHAPTER FOUR
Journey through Darkness

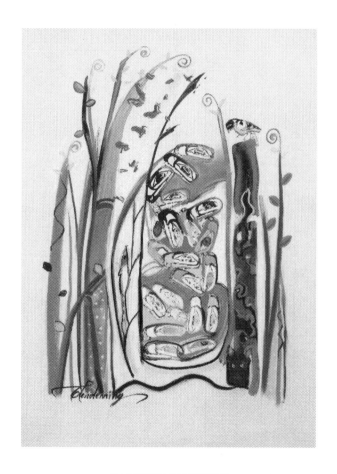

SACRED FOREST
© Susan Glendenning Art & Poetry

Great Spirit,
Help me know I am not alone
For You dwell within me and all around me
Help me know Your love that I may extend it
Help me open to that place of pure Being within me
So I may activate and know my higher purpose

SHIFTING STATES

Look, before you spans the morning of your dreaming
and your birth for all, from the shadows of night.

Storm clouds on the distant horizon signaled trouble. My uneasiness hinted the approach of great change. I would divorce in the next year though I did not yet know it, or the meaning of my uncertainty. For years it never occurred to me to question my assumptions. In fact, I was quite proud to be listening to my hunches and following my dreams. The time was ripe, however, for more learning. The time had come, to crack ajar the door of my heart to an even greater love and a powerful, powerful faith.

Ready or not, I climbed the mountain of my life. I prayed for insight and this vision answered. It swept me completely into its reality and felt totally real. In this amazing inner classroom my vision metaphor presented me with the challenge of shifting states.

> I was surprised to find myself on cold, narrow steps. A cement wall bordered one side of the steep stairs. Black nothingness emptied into night on the other. As if creeping from a cellar, I began to scale the cement stairs. On and on I climbed, until darkness and the unseen overwhelmed me with fear. Then quickly I turned and ran down, down, down the steep steps. Alas, beneath me lay only more cold steps.

Finding no way out and no end to the stairs continuing below, I huddled against the wall and shivered in dismay. How would I ever find my way? If only there were a light. Instantly, a warm golden light flooded the steps just ahead. Dr. David Alkins, a familiar friend and spiritual teacher appeared on the stairs and held a lantern high for me as I turned and walked back up the stairs, sharing smiles as I walked under his arm and went on my way again up the continuing and seemingly endless stairs. I felt tremendous gratitude for his warm smile of encouragement and the answered prayer. Once again on my feet, I found there was nothing to do but continue climbing.

The steps became narrower and more treacherous as I ascended. Ever steeper, up and ever on, into the endless darkness I climbed. But just ahead now, I saw a figure that looked like Jesus. He wore a long, white robe and also held a lantern in one hand. He walked easily up the narrow steps, while I found the climb becoming more and more difficult.

The steps gave way to stones... jagged, rough and uneven. Then the wall and the darkness fell away into dirt and rocks, revealing a precipice so high it took my breath. Others climbed behind us. But as this man continued to walk on, I had no time to look back. I needed all my concentration just to keep from falling off the edge of the mountain we scaled.

Morning mist materialized over the tree tops below. I knew with each second dawn advanced, bringing with her a bright new day. But just ahead, to my horror I could now see that the edges of the narrow path fell off, crashing down thousands of feet on either side.

My steps became so labored I could move only a few inches at a time. Then, clutching the ground, paralyzed with fear, I knew I could go no further. Icy desperation washed over me. But oh, how this master walked! Just look at him... so relaxed. Suddenly, I knew if I were to live, I must do the same.

I stopped trying and doubting. My fears certainly helped me zero. I drew in a deep breath and straightened myself. Never mind the how. My trust in his example was enough. I would simply get up and do it. I stopped clutching the ground and prepared to follow the way of this silent master. I shifted my body weight downward, relaxed and held my head high.

Oh my. What a revelation. I could do it. Relaxing enhanced my natural balance. I could walk this way. With not an eye to the side, or a thought for the depth, with not one look behind, but eyes directly on this majestic figure, then, and only then could I trust my steps.

As we walked on toward what seemed to be the top of the mountain, I wondered why... why had we come here? Almost instantly, we were at the top. No more path, no more edge, nothing. What would we do? As I followed wondering these things, right before my eyes, he walked off the edge of land into the air, lantern still held high.

In an instant I knew I must not stop, but trust and follow. With my first step into the air, a flood of freedom and appreciation filled me. More thrilling than anything I had felt before, the whole world lay before us. It was beautiful beyond dreaming, sparkling with morning dew. My heart sang as we soared. We were unlimited. We were safe and oh, so free.

How difficult and yet how simple shifting states could be. Help appeared in the form of light on the steps as soon as I became willing to go forward. A new world awaited and even my failure to understand the problem did not limit me, once I became willing to let go and learn something new. The impossible became natural as I emulated my guide and teacher. Freedom from the laws of my past thinking liberated me as I chose to live, more than I chose to fear. I was not alone throughout the whole experience, which reminds me neither am I now.

> Holy is the path before you, Peaceful Warrior. Sacred are the towering mountains of your heart. Carry with you the song of eagle as you soar above old doubts, old fears and strife. Behold, before you spans the morning of your dreaming and your birth for all, from the shadows of night.

DARK NIGHT

"You are surrounded by love. Ask to see it, and you will find it in every face you look upon." - *Dodie Jordan*

What a proud explorer I had become. Days and nights of communing with nature lightened my step. I barely touched the ground when I walked. Every day I discovered more beauty to appreciate. Nature presented me with a world so intensely delightful I wanted to memorize it, smell it, taste it and touch it. I could feel the harmony and splendor of every living thing's purpose at one with me.

My husband served a second tour of duty in Korea. After nearly two years of unanswered letters, I began to feel pain and disappointment lurking. I felt a shudder of sadness but pushed it aside. I had not yet become consistent in monitoring my thoughts, or noticed how bad I felt after doubting myself or another's worth. So the ship of my life swung back and forth. I did not realize I had a rudder inside me I could use and trust. I was waking up however, and there would be much to unlearn.

The faithfulness my husband and I promised lay dashed on the rocks of broken trust. I could not find my way around it. My husband returned home but my concepts of what I meant to him had shattered. Four years of distance, chilling silence and alcohol followed and filled all the spaces I dreamed of sharing with him. Instead of inventing adventures to share I waited for him to plan them. Instead of praising myself for my explorer heart and outrageous spiritual courage, I withdrew a part of my heart and blamed myself for being in strange territory! Outside, the summer air turned dark and cold. I scrambled to piece myself back together, but the damaged pieces no longer fit. I prayed:

> Help me, Beloved Spirit. I stumble. My wounds are deep and I cannot see my way. Shine your light through my darkness. Lift me above the shambles of my broken dreams. Reach out to me even when I am full of pain and refuse love. Help me become ripe and full again with your sweetness. Must I always wait for some bit of happiness to come from outside me? I will be honest with myself. I will not hide my feelings or pretend I have no pain. I offer it up to you.

I walked on, pointed towards the light, but our challenges continued. Without a solid base for understanding what I discovered, I tripped over my own concepts at every turn. So began the days of extremes; my joys and sorrows intensified. A single thought could send me crashing into unspeakable agonies. Soon everything around me needed to be redefined. Yet the irreversible process of opening my eyes, both inwardly to the beauty, as well as outwardly to the roles I was offered, had begun. I could not surrender myself to him with so much undone and I abhorred the idea of asking him to be someone he was not.

Our girls were away on sleep-overs and my husband and I had freedom to talk. I pleaded with him for soul affirmation. On the couch, by the closed window I tried to explain what I had learned. I told him how potentially alive I believed we could be. Impassioned by my new experiences I asked for us to become friends. I meant it as a beginning for building trust, but misunderstanding, anger and a harsh exit were my answers. Chilling emptiness hung in the air. Alone and silent I sat with only my tears to witness as my beautiful dream died. Betrayal, judgment, longing and sorrow filled me with agony. Yet, the awesome power of my desire to change and not allow fear to control my life, pressed me to grow.

Fleeing the emptiness between us to pray, I fell into my car and piloted myself toward the boat dock at McAlister Creek Boat launch. Sobbing my fate under the cover of night and into the receding tide, I mourned from the depth of my pitiful soul. I wailed like a lost child. I cried for help, screamed for help. Tears and sobs turned to coughs and gags as I emptied resistance from my being.

Quiet fell around me as I awaited my help. Nothing but my heartbeat seemed to exist. Parked by the water's edge, I watched the moonlit sky caress the earth. Then, a great thought penetrated my being: this moment so dark, full, and sick, appeared in response not only from this hour of need, but from all the hours of all needs. The pain, sorrow and loneliness were so great, they filled my cup. I needed no more. Truly, I could take no more; my cup overflowed. The feelings of smallness had deceived me. I was not small. My Spirit informed me, "I was a part of the All, experiencing small." In a moment I knew I was not empty, but full. I had gained a depth of passion and experience of sorrow.

This is the way I grew: experience by experience. With each new realization my confidence grew stronger. I would need it for I launched into a time of discovery and seeming danger that required far more presence than I had ever called forward. I read and sought validation in every spiritual reference even remotely similar to my experience.

My brother alerted our family of my spiritual explorations which unleashed a wave of family concerns and fear. Walls of conformity pressed me from every side for a better view. My family armed for battle and challenged my new wings at every turn. Peace no longer flowed between us and became instead a commodity only available at their price. True peace and connection however, were being forged in me and anything that did not serve this goal soon dropped away. My husband and I divorced; and I headed for new freedom.

My little duplex had a strange attraction all of its own; it boasted a great location skirting the edge of a freshwater marsh. Birds and creatures loved it. Many of my friends also felt at home there. It became a little center for healing circles and therapy work. I imagined our collective prayers anchored spiritual awareness to its site.

My husband and I would share the kids for the next few years until like magnets, my girls and I simply had to live together full time. Once I determined to get two jobs if need be, the Universe brought me a wonderful job and income to enjoy the heaven of my girls. The beginning, however, took some imagination. The shag carpet in my first little rental was another matter and required a special attitude of positive appreciation. Still performing after years of use, its Easter green color challenged my shocked daughters' eyes. *"Just pretend its grass!"* I told them, endeavoring to find something good. Other advantages I found: the wood stove saved me precious money if I harvested sticks and small branches from the back woods. One load of logs banked just so might last the entire night. No amount of attitude could deny however, much was still lacking. My gourmet Ramen, even when eloquently dished on my best china, lacked the main ingredient, love spice.

Whenever I grew tired of waiting for God to get down here in a body, I missed the subtle play of moonlight misting over the frog-filled bog. The shimmering aspen leaves had long since floated to the ground as I, unaware, let winter creep into my mind. But my shards of dreams, shattered identity, illusions shot with holes and a lifestyle shift so big I could not see my way, tumbled me to the bottom of darkness. My slip into negative focus attracted its own energetic resonance and felled me like timber in a clear cut. I tried to numb my pain with food.

How Far to the Sweet Land of Sharing

The evening fell as I lay down
Poisoned with food and digestive stress
Sugar drugged and drowning, yet unaware
Nauseating sorrow would sleep my body rest

So why write it, such darkness and sorrow
Why confusion, aloneness at nine

Have shadows of regret unharnessed
Lucifer's sinking thoughts on my doubting mind
Past life of joy, painful memory now
The shared beauty I loved so well
Where I floated as if on vacation
Opening windows to the fresh rose's smell

Yet lack of words and emptiness extinguished
The sacred life waiting there unperceived
In the meadow he left me standing
Trapped in ignorance could we nothing receive

Dislodged and weary from my journey
Dragging my body obediently on
In between the magical moments
Of bringing forth beauty, inspiration and song

Adrift and cast a sea before my calling
Yet beckoned and called without relent
I am succored by incessant longing
Sounded by some distant port of my intent

Mindless still, the tears of doubt they tumble
Grieving for a moment of delight
Stories and washed dishes sit shining
But what of warmth and tender cheer is here tonight

Help me, Holy Spirit, my Beloved
Come into my weakened heart and dwell
With Your joy that brings the morning
And a thousand birds to this sickening hell

How far to the sweet land of sharing
From this dark night adrift on the sea
When will the glad land come dreaming
When I open and welcome the harbor in me

Not, not, not, rot the old bones still singing
Chanting their awful, fading swoons
Rot, rot, rot is a heart so wasted
While unaware and alone under such a moon

Weeks past and nothing changed except for the crumbling foundations of my faulty thought system. Crying helped little. I longed for magic, miracles or a big eraser to wipe clean my heart. None appeared. Life may as well have ended. I no longer believed I could find peace, too much pain weighed against the door of my heart. As I began the arduous process of putting myself back together, the pieces of our old puzzle no longer fit. I fell to a bottom I had never touched before.

My friend, Dodie, boarded with me. Relocating herself, amidst a rolling sea of her own changes, we had grown strong in our friendship. As spirit sisters we had journeyed over many roads together and this night we headed straight into a miracle. We shared kindness, spiritual wisdom, Reiki and soup daily, to whomever of our friends needed it. We also shared a custom to pray, but this night my doors remained shut. Darkness escaped from under my bedroom door and alerted her intuition. My need to understand and be understood echoed like sonar up from the deep despair in the bottom of my heart. Sensing something amiss, she began to pray. Spirit, ever-faithful to answer, nudged her to get up and be the angel I needed.

Quietly, she opened the door to my room and knelt over my anguished body. I refused a response. What mattered? I never intended to rejoin the world of the living. I'd sunk too deep for movement in my dark sea of pain. I simply occupied space like a faint wisp of sea drift. Undaunted, she kissed my forehead and wiped the tears leaking from the last bits of my caring.

Bending close to my ear she whispered,

"You are surrounded by love. Ask to see and feel it, and you will find it in every face you look upon."

"I hate everyone who has ever hurt me, or anyone else." spit out my pain filled words.

"No one can hurt you, only what you allow. You are judging yourself."

Arguing for my pain, I turned away, squeezing tight my eyelids against the light, "The pain is still real!"

"You chose to come here for the learning; you chose the path. The pain is indeed a part of it; but beloved, the pain is only a small part of the path."

I pleaded on, "But I don't fit here. I don't fit anywhere. I just don't belong." But her voice of Love continued.

"You came here to make your place. This is your place for a while. This plane you chose."

Fevered from so many tears I conceded, "I can't come back, the pain hurts too much, I would only be full of bitterness and hardness." Still her voice of love continued,

"Your heart is soft. That is why it hurts when you put hardness around it for protection. Your heart is made of loving kindness."

Empowered by my friend's refusal to concede the dark reality I sought, I took spark of her light and began to heal. The long night of pain dissolved into day as compassion filled the new space in my heart. Any choice to perceive myself as alone would always be just that: a choice, clearly one that held no basis in spiritual reality. Yes, I could turn away, but Love's presence would never abandon me and I could feel it in every fiber. We don't need to protect or explain ourselves to be good people. It is an honor and a privilege to love the people in our lives.

In my journal I wrote: Today I dedicate my life to love, to bravely walking ahead into the unknown, to calling forth wisdom and truly living my thoughts of genius and joy.

I am always grateful when I remember that dark night of miracles. My friend opened herself as helper and extended love to me in whatever way Spirit might guide her. Afterwards, she did not remember the words she had spoken. But I remembered, because it was my Beloved speaking to me, across my chasm of pain, speaking to me through yet another aspect of my greater Self, my angel friend.

LESSON 78

The early days of my divorce ushered me into an unrehearsed stretch, one be fraught with glimpses of formerly unnoticed negative beliefs and issues. I had not realized my part in calling them to me, nor seen my closed mind. Mercifully, my intention to remain open kicked-in and I soon prayed for help.

Astray like a child with nowhere to rest, I plummeted into my friend Fran's benevolent care. Without me being present, my husband convinced our girls of the many advantages he might offer them, including solving the problem of their changing schools. My body threatened flu from the terror and stress, indeed the horror of living without them. My husband and my dialogue was still in such early stages I felt blind-sided. I had not even secured a home for myself yet. I loved Fran for the tenderness of her welcome and rested there. In the warmth and safety of her company I could let go of my need to comprehend anything. Though fevered, I fell fast asleep as she kindly covered me with an extra blanket and tucked me into bed like a baby.

We first became friends at a women's support group, in a downtown Olympia bookstore. I loved her immediately for starting the group, as well as for her gentle ways. Finding myself among those brave women thrilled me. I sampled freedom never before tasted; as I witnessed each bravely share her struggles and hopes. They began with prayer and ended each session with "Toning," Where single note melodies were composed on the spot, and sung or toned, by us as we sat in a circle. Together, instinctively choosing the pitches, we vocally explored whatever sound *felt right*. Traveling together through many emotions, we merged into a sweet consensus of peacefulness I can only nearly describe as the feeling of answered prayer.

To find such real friends was heavenly indeed. We vowed to be available day or night, should need for prayer or comfort arise. Never had I experienced such compassion and strength together. "Fill in the details later," we laughed, for we knew each other instantly. We recognized ourselves as spirit sisters as the essential part of each of us, our hearts, recognized itself immediately in each one.

In Fran's home, on that first night away from my family, Holy Spirit answered my prayer with a gift far greater than I could have imagined. Awaking from my deep sleep, the homey smells of hot soup and the kind voices of my new friends greeted me. Exploring the room with my gaze, I discovered velvet drapes graced the window. The comfort and femininity of Fran's style nurtured my senses. Candles and sacred objects signaled a tone of intentional reverence in the room. Feeling better, I sat up and noticed the books on her nightstand. *The Essene Book of Days*, a meditation calendar, lay opened to the day's lesson. But what really grabbed my eye was a luscious royal blue book, with the words, *A Course in Miracles* on its cover. I opened it, where upon these words leapt off the page straight into my heart.

> "This is a course in miracles. It is a required course. Only the time you take it is voluntary. Free will does not mean that you can establish the curriculum. It means only that you can elect what you want to take at a given time. The course does not aim at teaching the meaning of love, for that is beyond what can be taught. It does aim, however, at removing the blocks to your awareness of love's presence, which is your natural inheritance. The opposite of love is fear, but what is all-encompassing can have no opposite. This course can therefore be summed up very simply in this way:
>
> **Nothing real can be threatened.**
> **Nothing unreal exists.**
>
> Herein lies the peace of God."

I had always prayed to be taught without drastic means. I longed to learn willingly, before being required of it through pain and suffering. I saw no purpose in more of that. This book, with such a commanding opening, entreated my mind like no other. Already I could feel the words engage my heart for just that purpose.

The journey, upon which I embarked with the *Course*, would begin to show me how healing opportunities would be inherent in each day. My willingness to look on my choice for peace or pain was what the entire *Course* asked. I already trusted my understanding of Spirit, having a history since childhood of miraculous revelations. To test this path with my life would be easy, I thought. I was willing to listen. Thank goodness that was so.

I marveled at the sheer mass of words and wondered if its purpose was circular, to ease folks with doubting minds into willingness. I wondered if it were written for those who feared to go straight to the truth. Perhaps some needed first to dance over the many words, while screwing up courage for application. I would learn that every word bore purpose. In fact, the mind training program upon which I embarked required application!

Being an adventurer I had already utilized Voice Dialog, Dream Analysis, Tarot and Breath Work as tools to process my painful emotions. Some processes I even made up on my own. They all worked to some degree, as my high intention aimed at replacing pain with love. However, application of the many lessons, prayers and ideas in the *Course in Miracles* over the next twelve years, would lead me right out of time and space.

Now, four years after my divorce, painful memories of my failed marriage still assailed my peace. I made a habit of journaling my thoughts and feelings. Spirit never failed to help me find peace and I liked looking for insights. "Under His teaching every relationship becomes a lesson in love." the section called Text from A Course in Miracles had read. So, faithfully, I penned my regrets and pain in my journal, offering them up in prayer for enlightenment. Reaching for insight I wrote:

> "Perhaps our marriage failed, not because of my husband's broken vows and alcoholism, but because I stopped believing in him and in us. Perhaps I had given up hope we could ever find a way out of our pain together. Perhaps our divorce was good for us? Perhaps we would help each other yet?"

Yes, my budding soul awakening had been misunderstood, but nothing could stop the growth now underway. Help was on the way. I had lived as if everything depended only on my exhausted efforts, but now I was willing to try something else.

My blind heart continued to study the problem. I had not known how to let go, while at the same time keep the faith. I did not yet comprehend real forgiveness, but I was about to learn. Somehow I knew prayer would lead me to the true joining for which my soul thirsted. My desire to learn, to grow and to think for myself was naturally leading me into it.

> "How I long for someone kind and full of life and understanding to come along and love me. I wish someone would celebrate the magic and beauty of me, and give back a little of what I have given."

Innocently, I lamented for alignment I did not know how to achieve. I still could not see my faulty assumptions. My ideas of giving were totally askew. I assumed I had lost whatever I had given. Solidly entrenched in my ego perspective of separation and pain, I wondered if anyone would ever know me. My hope to share love again grew dim. Yet, God always opened a door when I needed one.

> "God help me." I prayed. "Help me believe again. Help me believe in myself and in others ... enough to live, enough to love again! Can I have it, Lord God of my being?"

Whenever I had prayed, an answer always appeared. Now in my mind came the answering idea to look up Workbook lesson #78. A friend, and fellow Course in Miracles student, told me this lesson really helped her make a breakthrough in thinking. So I decided to try it. Setting aside my pen and paper, I began to read through the passage.

> "Let miracles replace all grievances," the workbook lesson title read.

It suggested I might not yet be clear in my understanding, how all my choices were between miracles and grievances. It suggested I might lay down my grievances and look upon the miracle instead. Holy Spirit spoke through the words to my heart.

> "Go beyond.... See the Son of God, where he has always been ... He who was enemy is more than friend when he is freed to take the role Spirit has assigned to him. Let him be savior unto you today. Such is his role in your Father's plan."

The words continued, putting me at ease. Their intent was not to shame me for my feelings, but rather to guide my use of them. The lesson asked me to review both the good and bad of my former husband, his faults, the difficulties, pain, neglect and all the little things and the larger hurts he gave as well as his finer points. Then, out of this level of safety and honesty I was asked to allow myself to see my savior in, and through, this one whom God appointed for me. I was to ask my former husband (in a prayer exercise) to lead me to the holy light in which he stands, that I might join with him.

I closed my eyes and asked to be shown the light in him beyond my grievances.

What happened next cannot be written, nor in any meaningful way be described. I must at least mark the holy spot in my soul's journey, for the revelation that followed changed my life and all my future thoughts of this man.

> My field of vision shifted as I focused in on a silhouette of my former husband. The dark shape of a body outlined in light stood above me with arms open. As I looked at this

shape, the figure opened from one side, just like a door, a body shaped door! Intense light streamed from around the edges of the opening shape. In an instant both my breath and the entire weight of my body were drawn forward, up and into that light. What joy I felt, amplified far beyond any extreme happiness ever known to me! The light, white on white, everywhere moving in excitement, knowing me, gleefully greeting me, all speaking at once without being strange, exhilarated and satisfied me and nearly swept me out of consciousness. An instant longer and I would never have desired to return again to so limited a form as my earth bound identity of self. But the thought of my children spilled me back into my body.

I wondered if people knew this light of love on their deathbed. Oneness, as I never before comprehended, had been shown me. In amazement I read the rest of the lesson.

"Temptation falls away when we allow each one we meet to save us, and refuse to hide his light behind our grievances. To everyone you meet, and to the ones you think of or remember from the past, allow the role of savior to be given, that you may share it with him. For you both and all the sightless ones as well, we pray: Let miracles replace all grievances."

My relationship of pain no longer existed. The following days amazed me. Each time I made some casually negative statement about my former husband, the image of that door opening would reappear, canceling out any possible thought but wonder. My old habit of speech now revealed meaningless words, empty of truth, and served only to remind me of the healing. My heart no longer ached for lack, instead it overflowed with gratitude.

I am learning, what bothers me is not other people, but my way of looking at other people. Spirit is teaching me to trust my life. Maligning my defenses and making myself guilty for having needs or preferences was not helpful. To use my anger, pain and projections rather as tools, could teach me something I had surely forgotten: who we are: Love and made of it. Awakening to that was the holy purpose of forgiveness.

Today, twenty six years later, we've shared nearly every holiday with our children and our spouses. Love is shared all around the table. That is why I love my Beloved Spirit. What miracles we have lived.

For the readers reference All quotes are from: *A Course in Miracles*, copyright © 1992, 1999, 2007 by the Foundation for Inner Peace, 448 Ignacio Blvd #306 Novato, CA 94949, www.acim.org and info @acim. org, used with permission.

"Closed" - The Bitter Prize

Rejecting another but leaves us blind
To the brilliant light inside an open mind

Locked is the way when understanding is barred
Signs "closed, no discussion" send sharp daggers hard

When the night goes gloomy and pain runs deep
When promises fade in the heat of our need

Then tight is the door fastened close to the wall
With no opening for peace or to hear the heart's call

Then is the darkness far darker than fair
For alone though justified, unhealed we sit
With despair, our new companion, feeding on complaints'
stale grit

What answers can come to our voiceless cries
When blind to all else we repeat but sighs

Closing doors, closing minds...
Too high the bitter prize being alone and misaligned

But wishes become answers when to our Source we tune
We need each other for love's melody to bloom

Pray for wonder, connection and acceptance rare
For to usher in Heaven we must first be there

© Susan Flora Glendenning

CREATIVE POWERS ON FLIGHT 101

Prayer, my only recourse, did not disappoint
and called me right into a miracle.

Lots of major things had happened in my life over the past few years and it was time to go home and reconnect with my family. I had put my divorce behind me and dated a wonderful man. My new job already ushered me into great sales adventures. I had been awarded, Top Sales as *Senior Sales Counselor* at Panorama in Lacey, WA. I was painting again after a tremendous dry spell since my college and early marriage days. My warm smiles assured me I was ready for this reunion. I was genuinely happy for my trip home. But outside the airplane's window, gusty winds signaled, "Center yourself."

Wind and great cracks of lightening swept over the wings of our airplane. I normally did not fear flying and rather enjoyed the adventure of it, but this time even the stewardesses' faces paled. Up and down we bounced through the air. No food was served. This turbulence demanded I call upon my creative powers, and quickly. Prayer became my only recourse for peace. So, I opened my arms and my heart, took in a deep breath and relaxed my palms on the arm rests. "There, yes." Not a minute too soon as another loud crack of lightening slashed the adjacent sky.

Choosing to mind my prayers instead of the storm I focused on release and entered the sanctum of delight and sweetness. I began to give thanks for this great bird upon which we all flew. As I thought this, the most literal sensation began. As if riding on top of a great mount, I felt a bird under me. Then, through my closed eyes, I saw myself riding on Mother Goose's back!

I felt my legs hugging her sides and my heels pressing fast to her feathers as we flew. Within seconds the image in my mind caused me to burst out laughing, which made it impossible to remain afraid. The ridiculous idea thrilled me. After all, I justified, a grown woman in her forties should not be afraid of using whatever technique worked.

As I opened my eyes the turbulence disappeared.…. along with Mother Goose. My softened mood allowed me to look down from my tiny window without fear. The urge to write this poem grew organically out of my laughing gaze out the window of my adventure. As I floated upon success and oneness, my heart began to rhyme the phrases that described the beauty my eyes traced.

Let me amble like a river

Let me amble like a river
   Here and there along the way
Tasting fully of the nectar
   Mother Earth provides each day

Let me amble like a rainbow
   Reaching up so far & wide
Arms outstretched in tender loving
   Sparkles dancing from my eyes

Let me amble like a fluffy cloud
   That floats upon the air
Overcoming every obstacle
   And at home most anywhere

Let me amble like a rolling hill
   Curving up & sliding down
Tickled being oh so close
   To its family all around

Let me amble like my ink pen
   Full of joy and singing free
To the heart of God in kinship
   A part of everything I see

© *Susan Glendenning*

My joy and bliss thoughts overflowed, confirming yet again that I am learning how to access my receptive place where I can always expect to hear my Beloved's answers that help me, and make me smile.

A BETTER WAY

◆ ◆ ◆ ◆ ◆

There's got to be a better way.

I missed Daddy's flashing smile and my mother's perfect biscuits. "Remembering our love would be easy this year," I thought, as I relaxed into the flight home. Years of soul searching and proving new spiritual concepts had unfolded since our last visit. I stood quite tall now, without my cloak of many defensive protections, alas. I looked forward to my visit home.

I felt confident in my growth and ready to move through the fierce winds of my father's opinions and judgments. My sense of self-worth had grown and I thought I could be with him and not need to hide or debate.

As a child, I communicated with my father through a process of argumentative discussion. Sparring for fun, our love and respect for one another remained high, despite the fireworks. I posed questions, without committing a bias, which in turn revealed his opinions. He then, without need for defense, could let loose the mighty opinions he cherished. Never penalized for my unclaimed views, my ambiguity protected me while enabling him to assume we held passionate agreement.

Of late, all this had changed. The three thousand mile distance between us seemed more like a million. Daddy's second heart attack placed him on a strict and narrow path of health maintenance. He tried controlling his life with diet and great determination. Failing in that, his preoccupation turned to straightening out his daughter. My spiritual explorations worried him. Perhaps if he pushed me hard enough, he might save me from the world's devilish grip and bring me back into the safe shelter of his shepherding, back into the daughter of times past.

Thrilled to be alive and unaware of his needs and fears, I stretched for the sky. Full of experiences I could barely name, I now possessed strong, clear opinions. Daddy had not shared my years of processing, soul searching, and loving. Phone call after phone call, try as we might, intense emotions blocked meaningful dialogue. Nevertheless, my self-confidence grew hardy in a different garden, one enriched with my own experiences.

Over the phone Daddy had pounded away at me, pronouncing his opinions of what spiritual beliefs and rituals were correct, yet not one thing in my life ever fit into his mold of what was right. So, I avoided answering his accusations. I longed to be understood and tried to explain my beliefs to him in a way that I thought he would accept. If only I knew how to say things better, I blindly wished, then, perhaps he would understand me. What a trap approval could be!

In the recent past, we carried on for hours. I smarted from the sharp criticisms he offered and held my breath against the emotional shunning. I tried agreeing with him for the sake of false peace, knowing full well my thoughts were different. I thought the purpose of our dialog would be mutually beneficial and never intended them as a weapon. I feared angering him and did not want to disturb him, nor lose his love in the chaos that seemed bound to us. I tried to think of ways to assure him but nothing worked. I had not realized that sharing my honest thoughts and feelings with him might have brought us closer. I never thought of telling him of the valuable shifts I had been able to make and of the tender guidance I received when I prayed. Instead, I hid my opinions and spiritual experiences and kept silent, still unaware of how this built a wall of defense.

No matter how long the battle raged I always knew we loved each other dearly. This time I hoped our interactions would be different. Naturally I was surprised when my plans crumbled. Perhaps my confusion called me back for a test, or was it my Spirit unfolding strength that signaled to me, "Are you ready for more growth?"

How wonderful to be home again, I thought, as my parents ushered me into our familiar memory laden home. My mother's collection of antique teddy bears lounged on nearly every free spot. Though the guest bedroom's window shutters were fastened, fairy dust still sparkled around the tea set laid out for my old china dolls. The richly colored red, blue and yellow plaid curtains still hung in the kitchen's open pass through window and signaled to the lucky few, "This way for good eats." There were enough fine treasures in this wonderful house to open an upscale antique store.

Dad and I settled into the kitchen and watched the midday news from mom and dad's red, midcentury metal kitchen table. My high-backed black and wicker chair creaked of old cane as I sat down. Mother's collection of antique chickens decorated the table. The many nonfood related items gave a sense of adventure to the kitchen that I enjoyed. The large pewter and red milk-glass lamp cast a warm glow over the strawberry dishes. A bouquet of antique spoons spilled over the edge of a Depression glass sugar bowl.

Looking round the familiar room put me at ease but not enough to block the news of the world's painful news briefing. My dad and I ate bananas and peanut butter together as one more time, the black man Rodney King, was beaten by police for the world to see. "What a great medium for mass healing and learning, our communication system has become," I offered innocently. He immediately dropped his fork and swallowed hard. "What did you say?" Turning his head slowly, he glared, "The very idea? What kind of person are you?" His words grew louder, "Rodney King was no good! That policeman was just doing what anyone would do! We have to maintain justice through strength! What would *you* have, anarchy?" His angry words exploded into the room, propelled with disgust, and fell over me as sudden as a thunder burst.

Instead of acknowledging his opinions and answering him with my own, I ran to my silence for cover. Unable to honor him or myself, I hid. The thought of sharing how I had grown and gained insights from observing my own reactions to others' experiences never crossed my mind for I was loaded and ready to overflow on him. Instead of choosing my thoughts consciously, I reacted. I tried to protect myself by pushing. "People could learn from the story on television," I continued. "Aren't these scenes but magnifications of our own inner conflicts, acted out, for us to see?" Even though I believed what I was saying, my reactive words built no bridges for communication. Suddenly I was more invested in passing on information than in hearing him out.

His heavy load of fears exploded, "I knew you were crazy, you're mixed up in some kind of cult. How else could you say something like that?" His mind was set and needed no guidance. I got up and ran down the steep stairs into "the hole," our fondly named basement. I still had no clue about my defenses despite the set up they had created.

With deeply focused formality I maneuvered myself into a kneeling position on the floor. This was serious! I wanted every cell in my body to participate and join me as I prayed. "Dear God, I need help, and I need it now!" What was going on? Why had I come there? What was the purpose of such pain and separation? I pleaded to know. The whole thing was much too shocking and terrible for tears.

Only moments passed before the answering thoughts of clarity began to flow. Gentle peace filtered into the cracks of my seeking mind. The communique answered: I had come to reclaim a part of myself, of my truth. I had come to learn to speak, or not, but without the blinder of fear and judgment. I had come to learn to stay present in my heart, no matter what my father believed about me. How could I share my stories with the world if I were afraid to stand before my own father and say what I felt? How could I claim freedom for myself and not for him? How could I not allow him his truth?

Spirit helped me understand how faithfully my father had guarded his path to heaven's door for me, so the way to it might never be lost. Tears ran down my cheeks as I listened to my heart's wisdom. I loved my father for teaching me God was real. In our struggling we shifted our identification from loving, to protecting, and lost sight of the very things we protected. With judgments weighing us down, no wonder our issues increased. The sheer size of our burdens blocked us from entering Heaven's gate together. Unharnessed at last, my tears of forgiveness and understanding flowed.

Filled with gentle peace I climbed the steep basement stairs. I would not be offended if he did not understand my beliefs. It did not even matter if he called me names in disgust. I had regained myself and freed him. Now I possessed ample compassion for both of us.

Loving this precious man was effortless as I slipped into the rocking chair beside him and waited. Silent appreciation blazed inside me. To be fully present with him was my total will and desire. I no longer needed to hide; we both deserved love.

"I knew it," he shouted, suddenly getting up and turning away from me, "You are a 'new-ager!' I always knew it!" When I offered no defense he stormed away, leaving the oppressive room heavy with the weight of his disappointment.

The volatile energy between us however, had shifted. Just as mother and I were about to leave the house, Dad appeared from around the kitchen door. Facing me, with his eyes locking mine, he whispered, "I want you to know I do love you, even though you will probably never want to talk with me again." Love flowed between us as the era of our battling ended.

Tears of joy filled me this time, as our eyes communicated. A brook of unmistakable love streamed from my heart. Because I did not defend, and dropped my cloak of protection I could utilize the moment he gave me, an opportunity to be me in the highest sense. Without my judgment and pain I was enabled to see: yes, love was still underneath it all. Not one of our years was wasted, for we gave each other the gifts of proving, honing, and mastery.

I had wrestled in conflict with my dad because of the conflict within myself. Unconscious of my own confusion, I never spoke honestly with him about my journey. Until I fell on my knees in the basement screaming prayers for help in my mind, I had not seen it. Through the gift of connection to my spirit in prayer I was able to see us both clearly. My course of action became simple. I would be me and love him. Being true to myself did not necessitate him understanding or agreeing with me on anything.

Resistance to his perceptions, accusations, or fear was now unnecessary. I needed only remember my love for him. As respect replaced fear, honesty made way for honor between equals. Freed by prayer of my own self-deception, I could be with him at last. What a challenge, this gift, to see blessings through the disguise of fear and defense.

Now that his life here has ended, we continue through the gentle bridge of Spirit, to express the deep love we have for each other. I hope my story offers powerful questions you may also ask: "Why is this happening? What is the meaning? Why am I here? Is there another way?" I must seek the aide of my Spirit. Then I will receive the perfect answers, the ones that will return me to my heart and open me to my deepest blessings.

CHAPTER FIVE

Activating the Power of Love

MINDFULL REFILLING
© Susan Glendenning Art & Poetry

Mindful Refilling

Far from the tangle of pavement in town
My heart calls for balance
And calming things down
Where trees like tall cities so high in the sky
Remind me and call me
To glories I'll find
So I'm off to a circle of blue green firs
To cherish my planet
And re-boot my nerves
Mindful refilling is my work to do
As here in tree cities
I commune with inner truth
Lead me Beloved, your voice I would hear
And you answer,
"Tis only focus that draws you far or near."

FIRE WALK

Reading the Life and Teachings of the Masters of the Far
East transported me with a mystical logic so familiar and
refreshing I knew the miracles spoken of must be true.

Night melted into day as I read. Imagined sand gritted in my
mouth as one after another, the written words leapt as if alive,
off the pages and into my heart. My whole body responded. I
could have been in India. Spontaneously, I prayed.

Just what is real? If only I had such teachers, some master
with whom to apply these ideas. If they could live so easily
with miracles and even safely pass through a burning
forest unharmed, I would know this safety also. I believe
it is possible. I do believe it is true!

It was Nineteen eighty nine. I was comfortable knowing my mind and
living on my own. My quest to discover and understand the Spirit in and
around me continued. No part of my journey had been boring, but I never
could have guessed just how exciting it would become.

The following weekend, my friend, Fran, and I traveled to Breitenbush
Retreat Center in Oregon, for a *Shared Heart Retreat*. My mind overflowed
with excitement for the possible music we would experience. We both
yearned to escape life's roller coaster and awaken to our own destiny of
service. Our drive through immense forests, friendly log camp structures

and rushing mountain rivers lifted us into another realm. Surely past prayers still lingered there, in the sacred air over the mountain.

We arrived at the lovely old camp and went straight to work with other campers also setting up their sites. Twigs crunched underfoot as we worked. Happily, I ignored the bizarreness of our camping feat in favor of romanticizing the adventure. Soon enough the work was done. We pitched and staked our lofty tent and settled our spirits into nature. A feeling of wonder, peace and reflection exposed itself easily there.

Inside the tent my inner child, now an Indian princess, delighted in the arrangement of my treasures around my sleeping bag bed. Special rocks and my drum and rattle, pregnant with symbolic meaning, waited by the zipper door, all sentinels of joys to come. What people would we meet? What new songs would we learn? Humming with expectancy, we transformed our tent amid the clumps of bushes and towering fir trees, into a cozy home.

The next day, the retreat musicians, Charlie Thweat and John Astin, wove our hearts as one while we danced and sang our prayers. I loved every minute until someone stood up and introduced Tolly Burkan, the man who brought FIRE WALKING to America.

Chills of fear rushed through me. What was this man doing here? What if he offered a fire walk to us? God, I hoped he would be quiet. Then it happened, he spoke.

"Well, yes, I suppose we could hold a fire walk here if you like."

His words blurred as the weight of my bones sank into the wooden floor! In absolute panic I knew this was not a dream, but my prayer answered, even though the choice to walk or not, I knew, was mine alone.

He continued, telling us how listening to our inner guidance was the important thing. He told of people who walked against their knowing and were burned. I wondered if I would be able to know, through all the fear gripping inside my stomach. Would I? Should I? I decided to wait and see how I felt on the night of the fire walk. After all, I was perfectly free. No one I'd met there so far, seemed like the kind of person who would judge me, or even care if I chose not to walk, and no one would ever know of my prayer.

Outside, among the tall fir trees, the day dimmed into evening, but inside, the circle of listeners leaned forward, elbows on knees, studying his every word. He described a lemon to us and talked of its qualities until we puckered. He guided us to understand, that our minds establish reality for us according to our thoughts. He slapped his hands together loudly! We were to do the same. "This is what you may feel as your feet touch the coals." He told us. We could tell our minds what to accept as true.

I do not remember the remainder of his words, for I turned inward, talking to my Spirit. "This feels true, but when had it been my experience?" I allowed my memory to scan. "When has knowing something with absolute trust created safety for me?" Instantly, examples from my life scrolled past. I remembered the dog that stopped his charge on me, once in a field, as I knew Love and proclaimed, "There is no evil in this animal!" I recalled the time before a concert at church when my badly burned and blistered finger healed completely minutes before arriving at Church. I had prayed for God to take care of it. I smiled as I remembered parking places that appeared out of nowhere, synchronous occurrences, jobs, and precious opportunities to share what I had just learned. Memory even flashed of times when I had expanded myself, quite tall, up and out of time and space, even though moments later I fell back at screaming speed into my small body consciousness."

Yes, the man's words were very true. But did I want to act on them? And who would be the one acting? The Mind is powerful and untapped, but what would anything mean if this venture failed? Would it destroy my faith? What was real? What if it worked? Would it not demand applying new truth back home in my chaotic world? Did I even wish to navigate such confusion?

The next evening, standing outside with the others in a circle around the blazing wood fire, we watched as several men raked apart the glowing chunks of coal. Mist shrouded the hilltop field as the singular sound of rakes striking coal echoed over the emerging runway. Each of us reached inward for guidance and connection. Even though the heat of the fire warmed my face, ice raced through my veins. Excitement welled inside me, but still, I had no answer.

People began to walk on the runway of coals nearly twenty feet long. Tolly walked first. His little daughter of perhaps five years walked next. People walked and were fine. The entire group moved as one nearing the starting point of the walk. I churned with chaos and fear, yet on the people walked, across and off the coals and then back around, to circle the fire again.

Then, suddenly my feet carried me to the head of the line! Who did that? I screamed in my mind. I don't hear any voice telling me it is OK. I can't walk unless I KNOW! Then eternity dropped over me. I don't know how long I stood there, holding up the line behind me. I only know I began to feel an incredible peace. Praying to Jesus, I pleaded, "Please be with me. Teach me what I need to learn." It sounds crazy, but I knew it would be worth losing my feet, to learn if I could trust this Spirit inside.

Tightness gripped my stomach, but the dread fear was easing. As I stood in that timeless space, a most profound calm grew inside me. Was that my sign? "Yes! I could walk if I chose. I needed nothing else, for *Peace* was with me."

My eyes fill with tears even now, as I remember that walk. I glided like a great goddess of peace across the coals. They were rough, red and glowing, yet my feet felt no pain. Even as my heart screamed, Its true! a part of me walked in slow motion as I moved across the illusion of danger. Reaching the end, I required the use of all my self-control not to throw myself down prostrate, in thanksgiving.

My pounding heart raced as I rejoined the circle of people now holding hands. Materialized, and once again visible to me, their gentle smiles joined mine, silently knowing and breathing in the holiness of our shared moment. I was certain a cloud of angels, saints and friends hovered over us, celebrating with us as we stretched the very bounds and fabric of our reality.

My three by five index card, inscribed with the powerful affirmation, "I walk on fire. I can do anything I choose!" today waits safely, in my underwear drawer, ever accessible should I need reminding how every prayer is heard. Little by little as I dare to trust this something, not yet fully clear, but powerfully true inside, I experience the nature of our reality truly can be freedom, and our walk with Spirit unlimited.

The phrase, mind over matter, would be sadly inadequate to describe my time on the coals. I experienced so much more. My faith was strengthened, not in spiritual magic tricks, but in the possibility of real miracles. I would be forever joined with the peace and partnership, ever-present in my Soul.

Fran and I both find that a teacher or guide always appears to help when willingness is present. So dare to dream! I also learned we do not have to consciously understand, or know, what lies ahead, even what would be best for us, because partnership and unfolding truth rises from within us.

It is not the rituals that bring us potential, but the soul communion we alone must initiate that will reveal to us what is already ours in this great realm of thought and illusion. Rituals are but reflections of our alignment. Always our Inner Being is within us, ever teaching us and knowing just what we are ready to learn.

The next day, as I raced toward the phone to call my parents, sobering inner words of council and caution questioned me.

"Why are you calling your parents? Will this information at last prove to them you are justified in your beliefs? Will their knowing of it validate all the years of your life experience? Real validation must first come from acceptance and understanding of yourself."

I paused long enough to agree, and called them anyway. It seemed necessary to slow my racing heart. So, I was not totally surprised when I heard their response.

"Why on earth would you do a thing like that? Are you crazy?" screamed their frustrated words. To them I was disgusting for risking myself like that. My parents could only see my feet burning up because of some cult involvement. They were incensed!

Some pearls would have to wait to be shared. Forgiveness also, would have to wait for my willingness, until I would consider their vantage and how threatening my experiences might seem to them. Fortunately, Love can always be shared because Love is what is real, and Love need never wait.

Tolly Burkan and Mark Bruce Rosi wrote in their book – *Dying to Live*: "Five months ago I walked on fire, red hot coals to be more exact. A chemical engineer who brought a special thermometer to measure their temperature reported that the instrument began to melt when the heat reached 850 degrees. My feet however, didn't even blister...Minutes after I walked across the burning coals, I realized that the experience, amazing as it was, was not important in itself but rather as a concrete example of the ability we all have to do things we may not feel we can do."

Reprinted from DYING TO LIVE
Copyright 1984 by Tolly Burkan and Mark Bruce Rosi

UNLIMITED

W arm afternoon light and the scent of lavender filled the small upstairs Reiki classroom. My offer to assist my friend Dodie by auditing her second degree class already had given me more than I could return. I loved feeling the positive energy in the room, and never grew satiated of feeling Spirit's presence flowing through me. My familiar tears affirmed it. To sit in a circle with others also embracing love and The Presence was a heady honor.

As the class neared its end, Dodie gifted each person with an attunement. The dictionary definition of attunement, in —*YourDictionary*.com describes an attunement as a spiritual connection of a recipient by a teacher to a particular Spiritual energy …such as the Reiki or Universal Love energy. The student is then able to use that energy for healing. I bowed my head, closed my eyes and opened my heart. One by one Dodie placed her hands on our heads and prayed. Warmth flowed from her hands and bathed me in serenity.

Dodie's kind heart, strong faith and years of Reiki experiences allowed her to drop aside her ego personality and to make way for a bright bridge of love. As Dodie laid her hands over my head for the attunement these heavenly thoughts flashed into my mind:

> Joined in thought with You, I am the Way, and everything in my life, no matter how small in detail, is also part of that Way, that holiness - Sacred breath, sacred life, now for all, in all.

The thoughts filled me and transmitted a concept larger than individual words. The feeling of oneness unified every facet of my life. The thoughts sounded like my words, yet from another part of me, *my Self.* My best comprehension told me this was my Christ consciousness, speaking to me, for me, and even through me, all at the same time and with the same meaning for all people. In that instant, I understood how underneath the random thoughts of each day lies the life of which we are all a part. There we are joined in God and to each individual in eternal bonds. I realized how everything mattered as it related to that great Center of love and connection.

The tender oneness I felt, knew and expected, now promised to be with me forever, relevant to even the smallest details of my life. Overwhelmed with grace, how could I not extend this joy, patience, passion and healing grace to others? How could this revelation not expand outwardly through my daily life, reinforcing the power of our Oneness, the power of the Mind? No matter the concepts upon which my spiritual beliefs were based, I was about to learn the power of unabashed agreement, focus and alignment with a thought. How my faith in love would be sufficient to show me my way.

The next day, some of these same friends met at a local coffee shop. After grazing on desserts, we relaxed and chatted merrily at our little corner table. The combination of our bright smiles and the smoothly glistening, epoxied table top, must have bounced an invitation to the heavens, inviting angels and interested beings to come, fill the room. Original art decorated the walls and tickled us as did the traces of our once artful cuisine that lingered on our plates, now as evidence of our afternoon indulgence. Chocolate, rowdy birthday cards and philosophy combined well for us because we dared bare and share our emotions, our best thoughts, processes and healing moments.

Absently touching her neck, Rebecca discovered her necklace was missing. This very special necklace had been a recent birthday gift from all of us. Of simple design, the smooth silver female figurine held a sphere of deep purple amethyst high over her head. The necklace represented mastery and the willingness to step out of self-doubt so familiar in her past, to really live the freedom and love she espoused in her choices each day.

But now, only days later, the strong symbol of mastery was gone. Baring her soul, my friend cried aloud her disappointment, "Can't I do anything right?"

Immediately, all eyes and hearts turned to her in shock and concern. "Nothing that is truly yours can be lost," I offered.

She drew in a deep breath and weighed her thoughts, "Well, I suppose-" Then falling back into her doubt and sorrow, forsaking her power to know and hold the thought I offered, she insisted, "But it could be anywhere!"

The chain had broken during a beach picnic at Tolmie State Park. She recalled removing the necklace and slipping it into her coat pocket. Rebecca also remembered dropping her coat onto the rocky beach while we played in the outgoing tide.

"It could be anywhere now. It could have fallen out and washed away in the tide. It could have fallen out later in town. It could be anywhere!"

I valued the symbol's meaning and refused to let my dear friend lose a part of herself to a mere circumstance, so I told her a story: Stephanie, another of our friends, had lost her new watch. Rousing us from our heavenly potluck stupor, she had panicked in the same way as Rebecca had, but then quickly asked all of us to help. As everyone began to search, I closed my eyes, said a prayer, and then just "saw" it, in my mind. It was under the bedside table. Running to look, she cried, "Yes!" It was there!

Surely, Rebecca could do the same. She could say a prayer and then listen for insight about where it lay. "It is not lost if you say it is not." I continued. "Either it will return to you, or Spirit will help you find it." Was she willing to do this? She agreed to try as we exited the restaurant.

Outside the restaurant, the evening sky blazed pink and saturated the building's concrete walls and crevices with color. The normally mundane city street corner now glowed from the sun's journey over its walls and radiated warmth. Rebecca turned toward me, touching my sleeve. From her heart's dive into my eyes, I saw she feared trying it alone. "Would you help me look for it?" her voice quivered.

She would look in her car, office and houseboat. Because I lived close, I would search the rocky beach. Hugging with tears of hope and passion for spiritual truth, we each set out upon our journey of discovery.

The next day, Helen, my curious and supportive friend, rode with me out to the empty beach. She did not speak, so not to place doubt or fear on the clear pathway of faith upon which we walked. The salty air, pungent with seaweed, amplified the echoes of our footsteps as we journeyed over the long wooden bridge to the beach entrance. As our feet touched the rolling gravel path, the strand of beach flung her bounty of rocks before us.

Low tide invited the span of beige and green to dance and sparkle. Outward for hundreds of yards on either side of us, rocks twinkled, "Hello." Undaunted, confident of my clarity, I walked. No thoughts of fear or failure, no confusion or self-awareness dared come near. With steady gate I walked, as if in a trance I merged into the mystery of my Spirit's unlimited help. Like a princess in her kingdom of abundance, ordering a fine dinner, I extended my concept of reality and stepped into the certainty of my soul. Tall with confidence, calm yet excited by the power of Spirit's abundant love and faith in us, I paused a moment and faced the ocean. With head high, I walked straight ahead for perhaps twenty feet until it felt right to stop. Solid, like an ancient tree, I planted my feet and sent down my spirit roots into the jagged rocky beach and looked down. There between my feet lay the necklace, glistening among the smooth black rocks.

My work is to discover who I am, to keep my mind clear of doubt and tuned to love so I may hear and speak the gifts of my soul. This is my real work. Each time I connect with someone and see our needs as no different, my understanding grows clearer. We are all on our way to a new world, one seen through forgiveness' eyes. I am beginning to recognize this combination of Spirit and flesh is who we are. It has always lived in us, and always guides us. It is our work to commune and to find the symbols and signals that work for us to connect us and then to allow Spirit's unconditional love to flow through every situation.

Perhaps it doesn't matter what we pray for, only that we are willing to open our hearts to Love. Perhaps on our way to that sweet threshold of understanding, which Jesus, Buddha and others have known, we also will drop our judgments and finally rediscover Love's kingdom in us, and know why there can be no lack in it.

TRANSFIGURING PRAYER

I t was 1988 and finally my birthday had arrived. I prepared myself for a special ceremony by starting a bath. I had heard that one's prayers and proclamations would be especially powerful if prayed at the time and anniversary of our birth.

The kids were off for High School and the house, emptied of the morning's recent bustling, fell quiet. My day, still soft from the early sun and my children's warmth, had barely begun, yet my anticipation for the adventure ahead led me up the stairs nearly without the aid of my feet. My giddy heart luxuriated in the golden autumn light filtering through the fir trees into my bedroom. I did not know for what I would pray. I did not care. I only readied for my happy leap into the bright, liquid light of Spirit's love.

I turned off the water, dropped my gentle frame onto the side of my bed and began pulling off my socks. A breeze floated in from my open window and the combination of cool air and warm sun felt heavenly on my bare skin. I dropped my arms to my lap, drew in a deep cleansing breath and melted into a grateful prayer. My surroundings faded from sight as time slipped its cogs of routine.

As if watching a movie in 3-D I began to perceive a startling depiction of humanity's painful path away from its wisdom link inside. My birth year and even the particular century became irrelevant as scenes of human life scrolled across the fresh canvas of my mind. These tumbling thoughts overflowed from my heart in strange words as if an older, wiser aspect of me were speaking.

> "Oh sorrow, sorrow for the suffering of untold ages. Spirit awaits you. Always guiding, longing to join. Spirit lives in you, with you and through you. Know it. A bridge across the ages am I, across the agonies of love believed crushed. So much suffering, all from preferring the heartbreak of illusion, grand ego king of death."

I watched humankind absorb itself so completely in the outer, physical world that it became our only perception of reality. I watched this enlivened form of clay puff itself up, proud and fiery, fully owning its form and seeming powers, but I also felt a deep sorrow. Most had denied their Spirit for a focus on power and greed. In ignorance, most cut themselves off from even perceiving their access to Spirit and lived in sorrow.

I grew sadder as the scenes of suffering continued to scroll. Mothers losing sons, lovers losing lovers, children without loving parents or protection of love, the magnitude of it all overwhelmed me. I collapsed to the floor. Our focus on faulty beliefs and limitations spun nightmares backwards into history and forwards into the future. Overwhelmed by the communication, I grasped at the carpet beneath me and sobbed. The sorrow however, rather than ending my story, opened me to my beginning, for as I crawled weeping across the history of my soul, down the hallway of my house now a time-tunnel of collective pain, my awareness drew me nearer to our home, to the living waters of Soul and Source, where everything that exists is understood and loved.

From my deepest core I prayed, "God help us!" Then, imprinted messages of love, also laid down century after century, began to file through my mind. Unable to walk, now sobbing for the preponderance of love still being extended, and still naked and somehow conscious of both worlds, I made my way to the bath. The names of presidents, poets, saints and heroes, thoughts of kindness, all flashed through my mind. Love lit the scope of history, ever emerging, traveling with us wherever we might go.

The progression continued, ever ripening new triggers to inner doorways, ever prepared for whenever we might stop and return our hand to Spirit's.

I stepped into the water in perfect alignment with my Spirit. My body of its own volition settled me into a lotus position. A garland of energy descended over my head as I accepted and became aware of the union of my conscious, physical self and my infinite non-physical self. A vast, timeless certainty moved through my arms and hands as I baptized myself and gave thanks for our oneness.

What happened next was nearly unspeakable. The mystery of my spirit and my physical identity-self being one and joined, became a truth I knew and understood, as were the promises I made in those timeless moments. Again hearing as if to myself and from my Self at the same time, these words rang out.

> "Awaken to Source, thy guidance. Find each moment sufficient unto thee. Cleanse now the dreams of sorrow and memories past. In love it is blest and now holy having called forth its answers. The depth of thy being is vast and full of glory. Union of Spirit-fire, illusion-clay, knowing-feeling, unites in utter bliss."

> Then I answered, "Holy, holy, I lift my hand to symbolize Thee Spirit, and with water for thy essence Mother Earth. Love, I honor thee. Out of this center of brilliance the Christ energy in me is now birthed and radiant with light and love. Be holy unto thy seed in all. I now receive my Spirit."

No longer merely sitting in a tub of water, I floated in timeless space, connected and connecting to all people, in all time-flows. I could see myself transparent but for the radiant grids of light silhouetting my form. Awareness of body density all but disappeared. All dimensions awakened to my Soul's words as blended love beamed a flow of energy and blessing out through my open palms.

I dedicated my life in whatever way it might unfold, for the highest learning of all. I offered my life, my lessons and my experiences to be witnessed and used by any, who through them might better understand and claim their own.

The cost of believing this world is the only reality staggered me. Fearful reasoning and justification for lack and dis-ease of any kind stems not from an angry or scary God, for I can feel a host of joy filled, singing, jubilant hearts and voices reaching out to meet my stretch. The climb up through our fearful logic is the dreaded deed. Many prefer to stay blind. I was to understand our human part is absolutely essential in the formula for our healing rescue. Our willingness to love unconditionally will awaken our perception of Spirit's purpose in us, our union and joy, active and restored.

My original intention that morning came from my desire to mediate during the exact moment of my birth time. As my gaze fell on the clock, I realized I had forgotten all about timing my prayer. When I looked at the clock I remembered the three hour time zone difference from where I was born to where I now lived. The time aligned perfectly. Once again my Spirit showed me alignment perfection and birthday perfection!

That night after tucking my daughters into bed I wandered outside in the moonlight to ponder my experience. The driveway rocks crunched under my footsteps and stars bigger than golf balls nestled themselves gratefully into the night's perfumed embrace. Beauty sparkled all around and even included me in the night's embrace of stars.

I felt such reverence standing out under the stars, especially spirit's eager emphasis that I realize our equality in this relationship. I was to know we remain connected to each other. When our thoughts and corresponding energies are aligned, we will be able to tune and commune at will. Also... anything less will pale in comparison.

The days that followed remained profoundly silent of human speech, yet rich with the echoes of my Spirit and my promise to the deep mystery of my sacred self.

HEALING IN THE VALLEY
OF THE SHADOW

I reach my hand out to you, Sweet Mystery beyond my thinking mind.
I am not afraid to look upon you, even though my eyes are blind!

Clutching at the stair rail enough to drag myself up to my daughter's apartment and into the bathroom, I wondered if I had some kind of food poisoning. The pain of simply lifting myself out of my car had been excruciating. Surely exploding poisons now released their mischief inside my stomach.

Later that evening, back home in my bed, I diverted my thoughts of pain by listening to a cassette tape of Kenneth Wapnick discussing Jesus and *A Course in Miracles*. He spoke about how we project our pain onto others and perceive our world through the filter of our beliefs. He even suggested what we believe about Jesus, we also believe of ourselves!

Turning inward to observe I saw, yes, I did believe Jesus to be a victim of humankind, sacrificing and suffering. I turned in horror, to see my own beliefs about myself projected out over my life experience. I saw how the major pains in my life had come from seemingly outside events, words, opinions or actions of others. The list of examples seemed endless. I saw betrayal, disapproval, lack of appreciation, surprise attacks. Suddenly my blinders and defenses dropped; all the feelings I had hidden, stood before me clearly. I literally could not stomach what I saw.

In my personal life I wrestled with my own demons. One of my friends counseled me that without a plot, this book I was writing did not warrant further editing by her. My life seemed pointless after the rejection because I did not have a clue what to do. This book, albeit still more poetry than story, was nevertheless still crystalizing in my mind. It was nineteen hundred and ninety three and many years would pass before I would understand the part my passion might play. I really wanted my life to be of benefit, but for now it remained only a dream.

Just now only pain spoke to me, demanding, stabbing and engulfing me with its agony, even more than I cared to admit. I needed more love and trust than I had called on before. I knew I could not solve this problem alone.

My dear house mate and friend, Helen, put her hands on my head and prayed for Love to flow. The loving touch eased my resistance to the pain, however the illness continued, relentlessly ignoring our efforts. I became sicker and sicker. What if it were E coli? Finally, dehydrated and unable to walk, I acquiesced and called my former husband to pick me up and drive me to the military hospital.

Too weak for movement, I embraced the scene with my eyes and beamed love over the room of people. Children entertained themselves by crawling under their chairs, while the weary patients, doctors and nurses performed their tasks as best they could. Such gentleness transpired. Soon the kind staff had admitted me, administered IV fluids and given me a whole battery of tests. The doctors and nurses always apologized before performing some painful procedure on me.

Tommy stayed with me through all but the X-rays, pelvic, rectal and catheterization processes, patiently rubbing my head. I cried grateful tears for the support. Clearly kin for life, the five years since our divorce dissolved in kindness. My appearance, certainly as gray and ugly as possible, hindered nothing from the playing out of our timeless roles of tenderness. From his calm eyes I could only see heaven reflecting back our giving.

Awareness of my surroundings blurred in this emergency ward room, as a spinal tap was administered to someone on my right, a tube slid up the nose of someone on my left. We all seemed caught in a web of pain without meaning.

With five doctors, several nurses and a number of orderlies pushing, gauging, sticking and probing my already cramping abdomen, I longed for rest. The cold IV fluid dulled my pain, but rattled my teeth and shivered my bones. I thought to myself, "Certainly I would recover if this testing would stop." Suddenly appearing from around the curtain, in bounced the cowboy doctor with a scalpel on his hip. His cocky eyes flashed. His red hair matched the freckles on his arms. Descending onto the side of my bed, he asked for my age. I whispered, "Forty-four." Dropping his chart into his lap he laughed and replied, "Oh, that's your problem; you need a rebuild!"

I closed my eyes and did not laugh. He had come to question the previous doctors' work, and repeated the probing once more. "See," he turned to his student, "There's a mass! You didn't see that?" he taunted.

Interrupting him I pleaded, "If you'll give me a moment, I'll try to relax it. It's cramping from the probing." But by then, the other doctor was probing also.

"We need to admit you upstairs where we can take a look inside your stomach," he announced. Then, from the look on my face he comforted, "Oh, don't worry, just a CAT-scan and possible exploratory surgery." He then conferred to his student, "It's slow upstairs, not much going on."

To me, it sounded like this would give them something to do. So I answered calmly, "I won't be having surgery." In amazement, he asked, "Why not?" I answered him, "Because you would have to catch me first!"

His brow wrinkled into an irritated frown. Sensing his shock, I asked for some time to think about it. I wanted time to think and to confer with my former husband. To my amazement, I found Tommy supported this doctor's proposal one hundred per cent.

As if collaborating, they built a case for a reality certainly not of my choosing. When I asked to go home, reinforcements of specialists flooded the scene, eager to convince me of the gravity of my situation. Failing to move me from my resolve, the frustrated doctor disciplined me with his glare and unleashed his anger, "Your eyes are yellow. You could rupture any moment. You could have cancer. You could have a blockage. You could die. We don't know what this is," he asserted.

I stopped thinking, talking or positioning long enough to listen to myself. My inner sensors checked my body. Yes, I was sick, but I knew I would not die that night. I determined to leave the hospital. I needed time to get clear, to review the options. Surely there had to be a better way.

What a ruckus I had caused. The stunned orderlies stood aghast, with eyes hollow and void of understanding. In wonderment, they required me to sign papers stating I understood that I left against doctors' advice and might die. My former husband would not sign as a witness, his way of showing disproval for my decision. Stubbornly agreeing with the staff, he feared the seriousness of my condition. Unwilling to cooperate, I signed the release papers and let my former husband wheel me to the car.

Full of comforting IV fluids, I floated upon a sea of calm. I felt more peaceful for having acted upon my clear decision. Long spaces of silence punctuated the gentle quiet of our 30 year affection on the drive home. We talked about my premonitions, about my not knowing if I had a future, of how I had not been able to at least imagine one. Now free of all but kindness and the kind of Love that is eternal, we shared a space of timelessness.

Finally home to my own bed, I hoped to rest and awake fresh with new insight about what to do. Instead, I awoke soaked with sweat and once again in terrible pain. I determined to find a better way of healing. Throughout the next day my friend, Helen, attended me with Reiki, a hands-on, healing technique of calling forth the Universal Life Energy of Love.

My tension eased somewhat, until dehydration and pain once more blinded my senses. Hardly any thoughts now, either positive or negative, were possible. Helen and I both grew weary from the increasing fear. Steadily I lost ground. Soon even I began to wonder if I had been wrong to ask myself what I wanted.

It was time for a miracle, and I was ready to ask. Seldom, if ever, had I prayed for things. Clearly this was serious. Suddenly the idea to summon our friends popped into my mind. "Call everyone here to give Reiki and to pray with me," I asked. Their presence alone would remind me of Love and lift me into that place in my mind where Jesus and miracles could be received. There has to be a better way! I don't want struggle and pain in my life by choice. Surgery seemed a barbaric, pain-filled choice for my fearful heart.

Right away, Helen had difficulty reaching people. Frantic from the mix of hope and exhaustion, again and again she dialed. Telephones rang without answer. Our abundant resource of healers dwindled as the hour passed. Even the soft candle glow reflecting from the whisper pink walls, could not hide the lines of worry on her gentle face. Certain about something for once, I knew it would be all right. "Whoever is supposed to be here will come. It need not be a large group, just the right group." Immediately sensing the truth in my words she ceased to make further calls.

Two friends I seldom saw were first to arrive. They hugged me, their love and concern reaching through my hysterical, pain filled tears. Gail bent over my weakened form and put several drops of an herbal rescue remedy under my tongue. My gratitude exploded into pleas as I asked for their help, for Love, for a miracle. I asked them to know with me that miracles were possible, that it was my mind at war, not my body.

I trusted them. After asking me a few questions, Gail pronounced as firmly as I have ever heard her speak, "You are well. You asked for a miracle and it is already accomplished!"

Oh, how like heaven her words felt, permeating my consciousness. I thirsted for solid truth and drank in the lovely thought. I wanted every cell to hear and respond. They worked with their hands just over me, at a distance of maybe six inches, while I closed my eyes and waited for the others.

Fran guided me through a meditation over the phone. She wrapped me in a pink blanket of Love that would always be with me. She assured me of her Love and would continue with others to send prayers from a distance.

Every time someone arrived at my side to nurture and extend healing love, my gratitude for them and the truth they represented overwhelmed me. At first I thought someone would say something that would cause me to shift my mind. Yet each prayed silently, all the while keeping their hands on my head, feet and arms. Awareness began to dawn in me how I wanted someone, or something, outside myself to do my work for me.

On through the night they worked, praying and feeding me crushed ice. I gobbled the tiny pieces of bliss as they barely reached my tongue. Certainly ice was heaven, and they were angels. Still the waves of cramping increased.

My friend, Andrea, a Reiki master and teacher held the position by my head. I gripped her hand as our eyes locked. Suddenly she spoke, "Good! You are releasing now!" What a brilliant concept. I had not thought of pain as having any meaning. I had not even wanted to think. As I swam in and out of pain, I also seemed to sink in and out of clarity. As she dialogued with me, her logic began to make sense. I could feel it inside me at work. "Tell me what you are feeling." she asked. "Talk about your pain." I began to glimpse my own logic. I was uncertain if I wanted to live any more in a world so full of pain and misery. Words evaporated in the air as I faded. But my intention had been set by my call for help, and my prayers were being answered.

I told her of the blankness I had discovered in myself of late. She laughed and said, "Honey, that's the void, that's all!"

111

I told her about how important it had felt for me to finish my book, maybe enough to have been born to do it. I told her about when I had first started to write, to transcribe the snippets of paper into a form I could share, the wind had whipped around the house, clanging the wind chimes, but not moving a single tree. I had said "No!" to my fears in 'eighty three, and now in ninety three, I was ready to do so again. Andrea suggested that this pain represented more than one lifetime's issue of completion. Inside me I could feel movement as I shifted into alignment with the willingness to let go, to release the fear and whatever nameless, horrific beliefs lay fermenting in my gut.

In the past I had realigned myself with Love by meditating. In stillness I simply sat and allowed Love's energy and concepts of Truth to flow through my open mind until they belonged to me. Soon my understanding would focus. I always asked Jesus, Holy Spirit and Angels to be with me as I opened myself to my healing intention. When I could feel the joy, peace and utter truth in my heart, I would then quickly interject the painful idea, person or issue that caused me trouble. Sometimes, insight would come in that instant. Sometimes I would have to repeat the process. In any case, I continued until I could be at peace, and feel Love equally for all concerned.

This process of releasing my false beliefs, especially when they were large and deeply embedded in my identity, caused me to gag and cough. Of course I also cried the entire time. Believe me, it was not pretty, this process of mine. Forget the mascara and get the tissues! I normally processed alone, prayerfully releasing my tears in the bathtub or bed. I could open myself to uncover my honesty in the sweet privacy of soothing hot water, or in my flannel ship, my cocoon of safety. My trust in Spirit's presence to guide me was perhaps why I could journey so deeply into truthful connection while alone.

Only occasionally had I processed my issues in a group. Similar intentions to forgive, release, and allow understanding and healing to occur would be essential. Wallowing in sympathy or complaint would never serve peace, as I presumed it. My kind of processing needed to be real and authentic, not pretty. I did not want someone to smooth over my fears, sympathize with my judgmental beliefs or lend support to any victim roles that would further separate me from others. I desired healers who would stand with me, who also possessed the willingness to look beyond their own errors as well. With unity of purpose we might uncover a glimpse of the great and Divine Being of choice we all truly are.

Usually my tearful release accompanied a cough from so deep within me, it made me gag. When my hidden beliefs released through my conscious mind, it always felt as if I were suddenly freed to know what I didn't know, that I didn't know! Once, such a release precipitated a physical response, so strong, I literally flew off the couch into the lap of my friend, crying. My strange experience helped me to understand the mysterious casting out of demons that are so vividly described in the Bible. I really felt as if some kind of energy had been evicted from my body, and so it was to be again.

But that gagging cough of release, that letting go of fear, that sometimes shocking, freeing release of energy, always involved bending over. I could feel it coming and it terrified me. Strange how I could feel that huge wave of energy moving ever closer, demanding my surrender and at the same time feel its irresistible calm. Even though I already experienced more pain than I remembered from childbirth, I tried to allow it. The healers of God were onto me. As if in concert they shouted, "Let it go!"

I knew the choice was mine alone. I knew the cause also was mine. I had become disillusioned with my life. Nevertheless, the presence of Love waited, ready to flow through me and to express its Truth in much larger proportions through a much clearer channel. If I would live true to my writings, to my prayers and to my deep knowing of my Spirit, I had only one choice, to relax and trust. As soon as I knew that, as soon as I could feel that one hundred percent agreement of my body, mind and spirit to allow the flow of love and right action, I was ready. Now open to anything Spirit would reveal, I screamed, "Get out of me, ugly fear. I want only Love in me. I need room for Love, only Love!"

In an instant, I found myself not only coughing and doubled over, but vomiting. My friends performed as if they were the most competent hospital staff. Terry and Helen maneuvered towels and basins like pros, all while continuing to extend Reiki, and assurance. "Good girl, you did it!" the group cheered.

From my peripheral vision I could have sworn I saw a black, feathered or furry creature expel from me, then Peace. This was the beginning, the turning point for my multi-leveled healing to unfold. I seemed to float as I lay down, surprised to feel so much gentleness. My friends resumed Reiki with their hands just inches above my stomach. This time I could feel heat emanating from their hands, and lots of it! Tears of gratitude trickled from the corners of my eyes. Assured by the heat, I knew something beyond my asking had engaged. I thanked God for their strength and love, for their powerfully hot, healing hands. Immediately, the familiar Voice of Love spoke in my mind and reminded me:

> "Beloved, it is equal that you bring yourself to the place where you can receive."

My Spirit answered me with love, as gentle truth lifted me into a wider dimension of peace. I no longer resisted the waves of diminishing pain or my outmoded beliefs, I simply watched and allowed.

> A skeleton rose out of my stomach and I knew that Love, my essence, would never die. Another fading pain, and I saw bodies, as from Auschwitz, exposed and rise out of their hillside mass grave.

> Then an angel face flew over me, reached into my stomach and lifted out a huge bag of mucous. She had no body, only wings, and looked deeply into my eyes before she flew away.

> Another pain, and I saw my belief of Jesus as a victim released. The image of His tortured body began moving. Soon I saw the image moved on a T-shirt. An angel wore it and folded its wings in and out just so I could see that my belief was not as I had thought. Jesus taught that

nothing we can ever do, will destroy that divine part of us, or Love, or Peace.

I saw a young child rush into an old fashioned kitchen with a basin, to greet her prairie mother, now entering the room with a towel over her arm. Full of motherly patience and joy she invited the little one to enter, "It is all finished, come and see the baby." The door opened and I saw a monumentally sized figure of glowing light lying before us. It appeared to be the size of a face from Mount Rushmore!

Next I saw a heron standing in water. I laughed to think of my stomach as a lake. Deciding to go and dance with the heron, I began twirling around in the water, with my arms reaching up to heaven in praise.

Then I watched myself at age two or three. The child dipped and danced, gracefully splashing her hands in the water of the lovely lake. She turned round and round until suddenly she disappeared under the water. I watched intently, alarmed for her safety. Then, cresting upon the surface of the water, she appeared, riding on the back of a dolphin! Yes! It was finished. I had rejoined the will of my Spirit and I could feel it.

My friends lingered in the warmth. Some even stayed and spent the night, ready to remind me of Truth should I forget.

Safe at last from the tyranny of my fears, I slept like a baby. Several times during the night I awakened to check myself for pain, and found only gentleness. Secured by a feeling of safety much akin to a mother's tight embrace, my mind refused any venture into meaningless questions about the future. There would be time enough for all Love would have me do. The deepest joy I ever felt now joined me in loving.

I was also curious how a day without pain would feel. How free it would be for gentleness, to interact and to give praise and appreciation to others. I also knew I must face the doctors once more.

In the morning only minor bloating, soreness and weakness remained. I no longer feared any procedures the doctors might perform. I truly knew my only purpose just then, in being anywhere, was to be love. I was ready to visit the doctor and put my family at ease.

Two of my dearest friends drove me to the hospital where I was again tested and released as an "amazing case." The day doctor had heard of my case from the night crew and already knew all the details. I told him about the four hours of hands-on healing work and thanked him for his kindness, and that of the other doctors. He said there would be no need of surgery, and only one further test; if I could jump up and down for him, he could let me go home. I did jump, three times, to show him the miracle.

Friends from all over began calling me to express their love and to congratulate me for accepting Truth into deeper levels of realization and demonstration. They even said I was blazing a trail for all to follow. Unable to resist the opportunity, I joked, "Yes, I certainly blazed a trail, one of diarrhea! Maybe I'll write a book about it and call it *The Path* and recommend that people wash their hands after reading it!"

Surely my conflicted mind, afraid of failure, confused the value of my soul with the acceptance of my work. Unaware of my own twisted guilt, which continued to send out smoke signals: "Look at me, victim of pain, I am punished and cast off!" I was hard pressed to believe or see anything else. Now I see faulty logic. What kind of God did I believe in, one who would allow sickness of any kind? My attempt only proved how God did not love me. How arrogant my thought, to set up the problem at all.

My twisted mind however, could not hide the Love of God once we called for it together. Because my design was untrue was exactly why God's love *could* heal me, or anyone. There is no separation from God's Love and we need no defense against it; for each loving step we take for truth must reveal and reflect some bit of Heaven back into our field of awareness.

Whether or not we allow healing to occur in a hospital, home or temple is not the issue. Our need is to open our *minds* and release all that is not love. That is our issue. Take time out when you are conflicted, if only for minutes, and pray. Spirit can use whatever path we will allow, to lead us out of our darkness, bypass our blocks and end all suffering.

How quickly such an enormity of pain was released. I am astonished how deeply into the abyss of illusion and pain I could fall and still find my way out, how lost in pain and fear I could become and still access Truth, how unconscious to my wall of defense against submission to Love I could be, and still find willingness to look inside for alignment. I believe my willingness allowed Spirit, in and through my impulses, choices and friends to help me heal. I am ready to look now with Spirit, on every projection unlike love that might come up. Let healing begin for all people. I thank you all. God bless you for risking to heal, and for walking with me through my shadow, for your quest to understand Love and your willingness to laugh.

CHAPTER SIX
Ritual

BIG MOON CATCHER
© Susan Glendenning Art & Poetry

Great Spirit
As you are above, so be below.
As you are in principle
You are in manifestation: perfect.
Be in my mind as the bright light of love that you are...
Let your mercy be known far and wide
Through our joy,
And so it is.

MOMENT AT THE WINDOW

Intoxicated is the way I feel, deliriously full of love and learning, Whirl me through the Universe, stay me upon some star. Tt is love that sets me free.

A true ceremony can take any form, I smiled to myself, as I folded the top sheet of toilet paper into an elegant point and stood to pray. We can choose to use ceremony to transport ourselves into an awareness of bliss and more. I took in a deep breath and reverently exhaled the tension from my body. Straightening like a swan, I commanded-allowed the abstract quality of peace to replace my busy thoughts. I stood tall but relaxed, and closed my eyes in my own odd, if not funny-to-Spirit-ritual. My head and shoulders when prompted always emptied me of the day's stress and stacked my bones into the most comfortable position. My smile broadened as I began to recognize Spirit's familiar, revitalizing energy coursing through my body.

"Thank you," I began, "For life and sunshine, friends, family, birds, trees, fresh air, for children, even those not yet born, thank you God. Thank you for your love."

I never plan the list. Sometime I might simply pray, "Thank You for the toilet paper." My intent in folding the toilet paper was to engage a state of appreciation. It always works and serves me well. I love the beautiful world my happy habits allow me to perceive. Later, just seeing the folded toilet paper triggers my delight to pause again, to relax into awareness of Spirit and reconnect.

Once in a public stall, I prayed over each of four different rolls, accepting the full communion of love, over again with each new roll. Giggling as I left, I wondered if any residual zap might bless whoever next entered the sacred space!

On this fresh winter day, as I paused to reconnect, the lines and definition of my personality-self blurred as I folded the toilet paper and stood to join my Spirit. Freed like a bird, my consciousness spun out through the bathroom window into a pristine world of unity where I saw life through the eyes of my Source.

Through an Open Window

Away through an open window I flew
on a waft of sweet winter air
Out among the fir trees and gray squirrels
among the green smells and wetness everywhere

A bird sang briefly a note or two
a sign and a greeting it was
From a mystery dormant within me
now valid and awakened as I paused

Deep my breath, as I took into my soul
the morning's fresh, cool air
My soul's appreciation lifted me
into a moment when everything was shared

Earthly time stood still, for I knew it not
as I entered the sacred realm
There merged and conscious in every living thing
All joined in delight and calm

Now the songbird sings inside my heart
of Oneness and renewal in me
Ever its message of union and peace
Reminds me my life is free

May loving communion be felt in our lives
Its magic at work in our hearts
For no one is more gifted, nor capable than we
to dream Love's light, here on earth, into sight

I understand how Yogis can meditate all day. Rapture, belonging and awareness of connection with all life are just a few of prayer's side effects. Prayers of appreciation bring a powerful voltage of bliss into my body. My heart's intention to experience God in thanksgiving every day, requires discipline, but in the doing becomes its own joyful motivation. To greet the new morning and sense the Presence throughout the day is a privilege. To lie down to rest at night, appreciating all I've had the opportunity to love swings wide the door of my soul to communion.

JOINING THROUGH RITUAL

Your rituals should always serve a purpose that is meaningful to you.

Over the years on special occasions, like early summer, Thanksgiving, Christmas, or New Year, my group of Spiritual Sisters and friends create rituals. Our enthusiasm and intimate sharing taught us to love and trust each other. Without consciously looking for it I discovered myself to be surrounded by a family of spirit and loving intention that will always live in my heart.

Overflowing with laughter, gleeful anticipation and road food our car-caravan of friends, Sisters and Inner Child celebrants, headed up the highway towards Ocean Shores, WA. Fran had put together an Inner Child workshop and I was her assistant in charge of music. Our rental house also promised to please and stood right in the middle of two major bodies of water, inland waterway on the left and ocean on the right.

Upon arrival our cars exploded with arms, legs and laughter as eager friends tumbled out of the opening doors. "Freedom!" echoed our not-so-silent greetings. Some people ran straight to the water, others worked in twos and carried in coolers of food. Everywhere I looked fun sparkled from us like so many suns. Everywhere order and joy surged over countertops and took form as soups, salads, casseroles and grilled ribs. Our Vegan, non GMO and Gluten Free preferences would not take hold for a number of years.

What a fun idea, an Inner Child workshop, we had dreamed up. For me perfection already appeared as I found myself surrounded by my family of Spirit and holy intention. Of course we would melt together in song and live forever in each other's hearts.

And so we began with a ceremony. Cheryl Adams, an Earth Steward, inspired quadriplegic and dear sister called us together for what she termed: The Warrior's Sacred Healing Ritual. She described her intention for it to be an aid to awaken us from our self-imposed spiritual sleep, to let ancient feelings and dreams arise by activating a cleansing of old doubts and to allow an awakening of powerful union with everlasting Love.

We began with some symbolic physical movements: bending, scooping and then reaching upward. A poem unfolded in my mind as we journeyed through the process. Repeating physical movements rippled across the room. A single drum kept time. All this happened as Cheryl's compelling script, (highlighted below in bold text, along with my emerging thoughts,) rang out and merged as our past, present and future became one powerful moment of Love.

"Ho!" We roared, hands thrusting outward, open and empty, yet full

Echoes from within me: Moments of mystery now unfolding from my memory and shadows deep. I call forth my passion fires and dreaming to awaken in me, from my sleep

"Ho! My heart is jubilant." Spirit merging, mind and body, in me moving

Echoes from within me: Arise from my subconscious, ancient feelings great fury and wonder buried inside. Arise before me suppressed emotion Reveal even the pain my fears would hide.

"Ho, I am released." Earth Steward Sister leading

Echoes from within me: For I call you to be remembered and transformed in light before my Source. Flow through me as we allow together the power of Love to be our choice.

"Ho, I am magnificent as love at last is freed." Alive, honest and deliberate

Echoes from within me: High do I reach now into my vision higher yet, my prayers as I activate my Soul. Breathe on me, in me Holy Spirit, my guardian. Flow through my seeking mind, my God, my Source.

"Ho, I give you my ancient dreaming." Allowing Presence, and the power of Love that is my choice

Echoes from within me: Quench my thirst, Great Spirit, Eternal wisdom. Be my experience within and without. Transform my tumultuous years of yearning as I shed my darkness and my doubt

"Ho, I release the yearnings of my Soul." Synchronizing heartbeats

Echoes from within me: I accept the powerful union of your love that within me now does shout:

> **Ho, my heart is jubilant**
> **Ho, I am released**
> **Ho, I am magnificent as my love at last is freed**
> **Ho, I give to you my ancient dreaming**
> **Ho, I release the yearnings of my Soul**
>
> **"Now with you, my true will expressing:**
> **Only Love,**
> **Only God,**
> **Only Source**

My dear friend's life here has ended but still touches us with her powerful prayer. When I showed her my notes she asked if she might add them to her future handouts. I am certain some part of us is still dancing together in love.

CEREMONY IN THE WOODS

Our home in God begins here and now, wherever we find ourselves, and cannot be lost, for it lives in us.

My heart soared with positive expectation as our Sister's Group caravanned up the coastal waterway toward Shelton. Kanaychowa and her husband had purchased the lovely eleven-acre property to preserve the sacred wilderness. An invitation rippled far and wide calling us to come for an end of year ceremony in the woods. Our spiritual assignment and program asked us to give some thought for what we might release after last year's growth, and to prepare a statement of affirmation for what we would like to bring forward in the New Year. It was December 31st.

We floated out of our cars, descended upon the trail, and followed our host and program leader, Kanaychowa. Earlier that morning, she had prepared a ceremonial space for us by singing prayers and gathering wood for a large fire. Narrow trails cleared for single file passage, now led us toward a beautiful clearing around a branching middle-sized maple tree. Not a word was spoken as we reverently promenaded along the narrow path. Our silent prayers of appreciation must have resounded through the thickets of bare trees and native salal.

The winter foliage washed by last night's rain revealed her ceremonial diamonds and cast them before us into each gentle step. Each of us carried a candle to represent our love and to symbolically light the way for others. The soft blue sky reflected our clear intentions back upon us. I dearly loved my friends, and felt very proud of us for expressing ourselves so uniquely. Some wore ceremonial *Healing Blankets*, made for such occasions. Some brought rattles they had made themselves, filled with prayers or special stones and corn. Our ceremonial leader, Kanaychowa, wore her own garland crown of pheasant feathers, decorated with beads that boasted a large crystal moon in the center. Surely angels, birds and the living spirit of Mother Earth gathered to our awakening presence.

We paused at the edge of a clearing to gather our energy and ready ourselves for smudging before entering the circle. Smudging was a Native American tradition we had adopted when holding ceremony outside. Two sisters formed an archway with their arms held high. One by one we entered the arch and prayerfully emptied ourselves of all but love, while our auras were systematically brushed clean by the smoke of burning sage and white cedar. Sharon Rose used a large abalone shell to hold the burning twigs of dried herbs, and an owl's wing wrapped in leather, decorated by strings of beads as her fan. What a sight! Sensory rapture nearly overtook me.

A Medicine Wheel, also a Native tradition, embellished an Alter around the base of the maple tree in the middle of the clearing. Special stones, crystals and jewelry hung from the tree. A rainbow of colors represented different stages and seasons of life. Indeed, each item was pregnant with symbolism, animal wisdom and such. The whole scene shimmered in beauty and fragrant cedar wood smoke. The spot was magical. Surely heaven viewed us as a merry band of cherubs blessing the earth with our delight.

The fire crackled and spit for joy in the crisp winter air as each of us chose our spot and sat down around or near the decorated maple tree. Some sat on stump blocks cut from giant firs, or on blankets, sleeping bags or pillows. A host of ceremonial candles from former gatherings still nestled in the soft soil around the tree. Soon to be lit once more, the candles anchored reverence for future prayers. Birds and other creatures watched over us. Two huge half-wolf dogs and a playful mutt joined us. The massive wolf dogs rolled around pawing and chewing on each other's faces and ears. Even the boundaries between species melted here. The little dog investigated the ivy lairs and under bushes, discovering whatever dogs like to find. Even Kanaychowa's goat made itself welcome with us. He dragged his tire tether into the bushes, snacked on tasty finds, and gently bleated his songs every so often to join ours. I could never have imagined such a priceless scene.

Kanaychowa opened our ceremony with a song and a prayer calling forth the symbolic and energetic truths represented by each of the four directions. She began by lighting the candles on the east side of the tree. We all stood and faced toward the East as she prayed:

> "Guardians of the Power of the Direction of the East, Eagle, winged ones, Spirit power, 'Wabun', spirits of earth, elementals, animals, angels, to all the powers whose spirits reside in the East, place of illumination, birth of the sun, place of rebirth, I ask that your spirit power be with us today in our circle. Lend us your inspiration. I am grateful for your presence here and I thank you for your attention."

Ripples of joy washed over me as I melted into Kanaychowa's words. Then moving to the south side of the tree and lighting all the candles there, Kanaychowa continued:

> "Guardians of the Power of the South, spirit power whose name I know as 'Shawnodesee', place of childhood, joy, passion of fire, I ask your spirits to be with us in our circle. Bring to us the powers of learning from our childhood experiences, especially of the passion and joy that we came here to know. Come coyote, snake and mouse. I give thanks for your presence here and thank you for your attention."

The outside wilds thrilled me. I loved to pray together in this way. Then moving to the west side of the tree and lighting the candles there, she continued:

"I give thanks and call forth the spirit power of the West, whose name I know as 'Mugakeewis', place of death, death of an old way of thinking, of the setting sun, of introspection, going within, cocooning, beginning anew, of getting ready for the new, place of the bear who reminds us to hibernate and come back in the spring anew, I give thanks for your presence with us and thank you for your attention."

Letting go, yes, that was my real gift. I could feel my soul opening to the oment's possibility. And from the North:

"I give thanks and call forth the spirit power of the North, the place of 'Waboose, white buffalo calf woman who taught us to love and respect all of our relations, place of wisdom, of learning what our life experiences have to teach us, wisdom, buffalo, place of winter, of being still, place of waiting time, of being with all our experiences, gathering wisdom, of taking in what we have gained in the spring, summer and fall, place of wisdom and dreaming, I give thanks for your presence and attention here today in our circle."

"Fill me up, sweet angels of mercy that I may bless with you." I prayed. Then reaching her arms up to the sky, Kanaychowa continued:

"Spirits of sky nation, star people, thunder and lightning beings, beings of energy, grandfather moon, whose breath we breathe, sun that grows our corn, rain that nurtures our crops, shine on us and bless us."

Then bending down, touching the earth, she called:

"Spirit of Mother Earth, send your energy up through our feet. Bless us with your nurturing. Thank you for giving us life and for being so patient with us. Send your nurturing forces to us in our ceremony and bless us with your loving warmth. We are grateful for your presence here and thank you for your attention."

After this we drummed, sang and rattled with full hearts. Then one by one, as we were so moved, we placed our candles in the soft soil around the maple tree, stood before the group and shared our releases. Then we put the paper our releases were written upon into the fire. When all were complete we left the woods singing, with auras wide and hearts full. My fingertips tingled as I blessed the plants along the way. As I walked along the glistening trail back towards the house with my sisters, I so wished I had a gift I might give them. As we walked gently along the trail my idea came. I would receive a word special for each one.

Back in the warm house we gathered around the wood stove, warmed our insides with hot tea and shared our affirmations and prayers for the New Year with the group. Hot tea never tasted so good. Next we made little prayer bags for our affirmations. The bags were red to represent life energy. We tied them up with green string to represent growth, eternal life and Christmas.

As we began to say our goodbyes and readied for our trip back home, I felt the familiar excitement and sweetness of my Beloved Inner Being. The time was right. When I first began to whisper the words to each one I never dreamed how profoundly Spirit's presence would be felt. One person cried. One experienced new clarity on something important to them. All were astonished at the subtle meanings and clicks they received, and on topics that no one else could have known. I cried too as I realized Spirit did not need my comprehension to deliver the gifts for which I had prayed. Meaning beyond me was present. Spirit was able to work through us all in meaningful ways.

Closing we sang *Alleluia*, my song of gratitude, a cappella. This time as we sang it we breathed our prayers of appreciation into each verse, for the earth, its children, nations and creatures. Our simple but intentional ceremony composed of love and pieces of this and that wove our hearts together and surely went out beyond our knowing, across the universe to bless. We sought Spirit's presence and found it in the cold winter air. I have never forgotten the magic of that day.

The next day Kanaychowa told me she had gone back into the woods exactly at midnight to delight in our ceremony again, lit our candles and prayed once more. As she paused under the stars and loveliness of the night, before the wonderful tree aglow from our lit candles, she began to sing *Alleluia*. Then, through the mystery of Spirit, though physically alone, she heard our voices singing with hers!

The miraculous wonder is we actually were singing *Alleluia* at the exact same time at another friend's house in Olympia. I still remember the holiness I felt as we sang that night. Spirit blessed us and sang through us. I could feel pure love in the perfect tones that floated from our voices. We had never sung it so beautifully before. Original harmonies co-created on the spot blended and resounded, distilling us into a heavenly choir that surely joined others beyond the boundaries of time and space.

Have fun creating your own ceremonies. Invent your own traditions with your friends and sisters. Incorporating spiritual practices from around the world, whether Buddhist, Tibetan, native American, African or Christian can bring a global unity to our prayers when we allow it.

CHAPTER SEVEN
Together in Time

PRAYER STICK
© Susan Glendenning Art & Poetry

I surrender to you, Love within me. Lead me to the true meaning of each day as I celebrate the beauty of each person or creature I am graced to meet along the way. Oh, such gladness to feel the loving, the simple pleasure of appreciating each one I see. Delighting in each glad greeting, I can feel Your peace again, inside of me.

THE GREATEST GIFT

The winds raged outside our log cabin. In my dream I found myself huddled into a ball of arms as my fearful family clutched at each other for protection. My mother hurled herself against the door, offering her strength as strategy against the immense and dangerous 'something' that thundered against the front of the house. Gasping for air amidst our screams of terror, we stood powerless but to watch as mother accidentally unbolted the door! Bursting through the heavy log door, a giant bear bounded into the room and headed straight for me, but, instead of tearing me to shreds, as we surely thought, the bear tossed me up onto his shoulders and began dancing me around the room!

Marriage would be much like that for me: full of great terror, and lovely surprises. I was aware that many challenges might arise on my way back to remembering love, in which I might not yet comprehend my part. If I would know a 'holy' relationship, I would need to call upon and live from my Spirit, and extend what I might want returned. I discovered love was not something I could learn, but rather something I would open to.

Single now seven years after my first marriage had ended, I stood poised on the threshold of sincere willingness. I realized room did exist in me for sharing and communing in love. Where this new desire would take me however, I could not foresee.

Stunned one night by another dream, I saw the shocking metaphor of myself as aging, as reaching my 'shelf-life', or the expiration date on my label, as if I were an item of food stuff. My shocking, fearful dream seemed to warn, "If I was not shared and enjoyed soon, like the food, I would be worthless even for giving away!" I decided to date.

My transformation from asexual Susan into *my name is woman and I am ready to date*, stunned even me as miraculous. Hiding beneath my calm and friendly smile lay a giddy, nearly forgotten young woman. Nervously, revealing this vulnerability, I discarded my oversized, bulky suits and dared to decorate this new potential with a soft and feminine dress. I didn't know a marriage commitment would not be required on first dates, so naturally I proceeded with extreme caution.

Upon entering the populated and richly-decorated elegance of the candle-lit restaurant with my first date, I was astonished to find smiles and raised eyebrows of appreciation greeting me instead of stares. What fun to meet people from this new persona of untapped charm. More than my walk changed that night. I discovered I not only had preferences but appreciation for the people coming my way. Each occasion evidenced a delightful new facet of me and my date. I looked for and found good reflected in each person. Finally trusting this to be an unfolding process of joy, I allowed myself to simply have fun and began to share the life I so loved.

All seemed to be going quite well. I prayed for the ability to embody and share all the characteristics I wanted to draw into my life. Each day brought someone new. I even met men in the grocery store! "Something quite chemical must be occurring." I thought. Nearly eight years had passed since I had seen such interest! Now it seemed I was ripe. Perhaps the blossoms of my personality signaled and engaged even far-ranging butterflies with my call for love. I did not know who it would be, just that something very good would happen soon. Like a child before Christmas, I looked forward to the adventures each new day might bring.

Jerry and I had known each other for two years. We both worked for the same Retirement community. He was much taller than I and as dashing a figure of manly fashion as I had seen. His flashing blue eyes sparkled at both the patrons and employees, and bespoke an inner kindness

I loved to see. Easily mixing wit and competence he managed his staff with his spirit. By simply being present, he brought charm to any room. He mentioned he had a relationship that was ending but said he had no desire for another intimate relationship.

Sometime later he told me while driving with his mother and sister, a revelation had struck him: *God was going to put a very different kind of woman in his life, an angel!* He said no such other-worldly thought had ever crossed his mind. Somewhere inside himself, though unaware of it, perhaps he also readied for a holy relationship?

Our dating commenced only days later when, as if struck by a spiritual thunderbolt, he realized the angel was me. Stumbling somewhat awkwardly, into my office, he made himself comfortable in one of my client chairs. We sat there in shock for a few silent moments then he got up to leave. I joked with him "Don't come back without a plan." Then he left. Just like that. I went back to work but wondered what he was up to. As I walked out of the building a little later, and headed for my car, he bounded from around the corner almost bumping into me and asked me if I would like to go out for dinner.

The charm and whimsy of this big man made me laugh and I didn't mind our ten year age difference. Also, he was the only one who had not fainted when I told them I loved to dance Argentine Tango. I did wonder how our very different lives would meld. He loved the city and I adored the woods. We both considered ourselves gourmet cooks. Being a hotel man, he loved five star hotels. I adored spiritual healing groups, drumming and musical retreats. The drumming and sing-a-long music of my friends must have frightened him but he stayed. The abundance of music I wrote and sang with passion never seemed to turn his head.

What kind of friend would I be if I dropped his friendship? I prayed to love him as God would, unconditionally. I decided to continue our friendship. I would not turn my back on him because of our differences. Surely no order of difficulty would be too great for love to handle or make right. I decided to let love teach me and bring up for healing anything unlike love.

137

I believe it was then, that my willingness and clarity engaged my Spirit to use everything occurring between us to teach me.

After six months of getting to know each other, trust and love finally overflowed the boundaries of my resistance and we joined forces in a committed relationship that grew steadily into our present marriage. And so it was we began our holy relationship charged with lessons to learn, issues to heal, fun to discover and love, the greatest gift of all to share, where miracles, daily ones, would move our awareness from differences to delight.

Love's Gift

Long forested away in the caves of my seeking
I lived very well on seeds of sweet truth
Until one day I longed and prayed to share wonder
To feel and demonstrate love's perfect fruit
Then you came to me
In glowing robes of your soul's opening
Breathing whispers of shared loving
So I dared stay present and listening
No matter how loudly my fears pounded away
Would this night of unknowing stifle again my glad day
But you kept smiling
Confidence spilling out from your eyes
As your truth spoke and awakened my heart
Tonight my soul whispers fondly to yours
Unafraid now, I love playing in your arms
Without you there would be no dancing
Without you the stars would not shine so bright
Without you my heart wouldn't know of its rhythms
Nor of the beauty I now see in your eyes
In you I can see the soul's beauty
Through your unobstructed openness
Creation sings to my heart and fills me with the blue sky
in your eyes

HEALING THROUGH RELATIONSHIP

Angels speed me along my way for my gaze skips irresistibly from my driving to sun lit leaves and the golden man heaven has brought my way. Now everywhere I look I see gold. Leaves shimmer all around touching me with the grace of evening. Heaven go with me for all the while there is a road under my wheels that seems to journey with me as I travel closer and closer to the music in our souls.

M any of my friends with the most wonderful relationships have told me of their having been through tough times to get to the calm, trusting place they share today. And after all, who hasn't acted on faulty assumptions, I asked, trying to forgive myself for getting my feelings hurt and quarreling with my husband. But then the real question remained, hollering like a wolf-chorus in my mind. Would I rather be right or happy?

Well, I didn't want to see that possibility leaping around in my mind. If I chose happiness, I'd be forced to see us both living and perceiving through our own filters of right and wrong, and thereby forced to see us *both* as right.

The clock ticked. Hum. If I pronounced only me as 'right' I would still have to admit we both needed some self-actualization and mercy. I could already sense by my, as yet only brief time of introspection, that the longer we dragged these battles out, the more momentum our issues would grow.

I could clearly see it was getting easier to judge! Already I barely cared a flip about mercy! Maybe I no longer wanted it from him! Oh agony, for these small problems!

Our problems were certainly not very big, just very painful. And my unruly ego loved diversions. But I was becoming weary and bored of our fray. This change in mood, I knew, was my signal for a start-over, our signal to make peace. It meant re-booting, forgetting the problem and hugging... sounds simple.

I hoped dissecting my thoughts would magically free me; instead it only made things worse. Heaven forbid I should simply *decide* to drop all problems for a better way.

I did care. I did love the rascal, but right then my loudest concern was who would go first. I knew it would have to be me. Oh poor me! Why? Because I was keenly aware how great love feels. I was also keenly aware how horrible being out of loving alignment felt! I would have to choose love; it was just a matter of time. Being out of sync with my heart was just way too painful.

My study of *A Course in Miracles* had taught me whoever possessed the greatest light in any moment was the one tasked to respond.

Sometimes Jerry would want to fester for a few days. Oh double agony! That meant I had no control over his choices and of course I tried to hurry him... which never worked. This is when I learned to make way for my own steadiness and secure my own state of happiness before tackling anything with anyone else. See how cleverly Spirit answers. It helps us grow strong and wise through our conflicts. We have gotten really good at hugging.

There are many ways to sync-up with our loving selves portrayed in this book. The Promised Land especially starts to appear for me when I feel myself desiring to write appreciations about my focused "opponent." So be forewarned, gifts often come in disguised packages.

For many years I carried a heavy burden; I believed every problem was about me. Now sometimes, I find the drama is not always about me at all; someone else may be calling for love, just like I do. Then I remember my job is to activate my own love by turning all problems over to Spirit to handle. When I co-create with my Beloved in this way, help in the form of ideas, people, solutions, means, talents and the miracles needed, occur. So don't be afraid. Healing through relationships can be an astounding, happy-making and holy practice that actually heals us all. Today my husband and I are more deeply in love than ever.

"Anyone can learn from these stories my friend Marcia, told me, especially when working through the hard parts of relationships. This writing is risky because one cannot hide behind false pretenses. This writing is powerfully honest." **Marcia Jacyna**

PUGGY CHIN

T he unannounced memory of Puggy's softness shot through my body like a thunder clap, and short-circuited my morning treadmill routine, as fourteen years of loving between dog and human cornered my awareness and left me full of questions.

I could smell her fur and felt her presence as if she were physically there. What purpose had these memories come to announce? I had not a clue as my feet stumbled and nearly tumbled me onto the still-moving rubber floor. As on so many other mornings I expected nothing more than an invigorating workout, yet here I staggered, nearly overcome with weakness.

Why now, three years after her passing, had she returned? I clutched the treadmill's metal supports and attempted to compose my emotions. I matched my steps with the treadmill's steady pace and marveled at the dusty, musty scent of her fur. It filled my lungs and heart and took me back to her passing when I had held her in my arms. Torn between feelings of grief and gratitude I prayed, "I'm listening," and allowed myself to dive further inward.

Shinping Puggy Chin, what a lofty name. Shinping stood for 'peace' and Puggy Chin, well we called her Puggy because one could see she barely possessed a chin. Her luxurious fur could ease even the gruffest of souls as she presented herself to any casual contact with fingers available for petting.

Gray and white spots decorated her furless pink tummy, making our family laugh at her bizarre clown costume. No wonder our daughter, Jennifer, chose her. To a fourth grader, Puggy had it all: the warmth and cuddle of a small furry companion, plus the adorable face of a clown. Her long and floozy schitzu tail far exceeded any practical requirements of dog-dom. To me, it illustrated the flair of a consummate artiste.

Her short legs barely kept her Victorian fur skirts off the floor. Bravely she endured all the grooming her life coat required, even facing the indignity of a 'puppy cut' through her mature years.

Perhaps she recalled royal ancestors, and hailed from a line of faithful guardians who maintained sentinel duty at monastery entrances. Perhaps she used her excited bark to alert us, her modern monks, to arise from prayers: "Come wake; company approaches the door!" She commanded such respect we dared not take offense at barking. My daughters and all my friends adored our bold Guardian.

Our frequent walks took us deep into lush forest bowers, shady with wet, leafy places even up and over our hillside's miniature version of the Rockies. She investigated every twig to be sure it would not present a danger to us, and galloped twice our distance, as she reconnoitered the path ahead then returned to make sure we were following along and not way-laid.

I smiled to remember how I had attempted to protect her from other dogs... for she had a "mouth," and felt compelled to challenge even the largest beast. She never considered her belligerent conduct the least bit improper or unladylike; nor did she entertain having that particular "rudeness" trained out of her. This was her job, and she would do it.

One day especially stood out in my memory. I had walked with her out into the wetland marsh behind my apartment planning to lie in the long, soft summer grass. One could hide in this and I sometimes fantasized bringing a lover there. However, it was Puggy who remained faithful and accompanied me on this soft yellow day. Frogs sang as she happily sniffed the tall grasses and explored anything hiding under last year's fallen aspen leaves. We rolled around heaven, watching story clouds trace their plots across the sky until finally dinnertime hunger pangs compelled us homeward.

No spot could have been lovelier, I thought. We retraced our steps home. Several of the tenants tended gardens along the lush, marsh edge. Puggy, of course, had to sniff there, so I carefully attached her leash. As we walked up the gentle slope toward our porch out bounded the neighbor's enormous pit bull. In a blink, Puggy swizzled her head right out of her collar and flew towards the approaching dog. Too frightened to think as she leapt into death's open jaws, I simply stopped, dropped my weight into the earth through my feet and screamed with my mind, "Angels help!" and to Puggy, "Puggy, if you want to die, this is a good time. It's certainly up to you."

Instantly, she and the large intruder stopped nose to nose. Seconds later the owner ran out, collected her dog and hurried back into the obscurity of their apartment. I collapsed to the ground and hugged my frisky treasure. She heard me!

I knew I could depend upon her love. For fourteen years, she served all she met with plumy wags and warm licks, her love kisses. Then one day all the wheels fell off her little wagon, and she laid her precious body down for the final time.

It was unusual for her to tread upon my flowers, but that day she lay in the middle of them. The cool, fragrant purple lobelia and white alyssum buoyed her throne, as our queen took her proper place. Gentleness, respect and gratitude stilled any need for spoken words. We asked the vet to come to our house, gathered Puggy's friends and the members of our family to stand with her at her time of passing. As the doctor administered the injection of sleep, we sang *Alleluia, My Soul Gives Thanks*, and prayed for her safe passage. She died, cradled in my arms.

In the safety of our garden we could wail our grief aloud, without restriction. As Puggy died, a piercing sweetness split my heart as hundreds of memories of her unconditional love pressed together in my mind's awareness. Afterwards, we spoke in turn around the circle of our love for her and what she had taught us. Later, when I looked at my notes and cards, they read as if from her:

> "Come walk with me. Follow my bobbing tail. I am traveling into the skies but you can still know me as the wind touches your face. I am here. I am in the rainbow's colorful leap. I am in the independence of your own self knowing. Greet the day as I did, with an open heart. As I found your love returning to me, so shall you find yours returning to you as you play. I will always love you."

Finding myself back on the treadmill, I puzzled, "Spirit, I still want to understand. I know the illusion of separation and death is not real, but what does this intense love mean? Who is she?"

Then as clearly as the chime of a bell, the Inner voice answered me, *"Didn't you know? It was me."*

CHAPTER EIGHT
In Every Medium

TOTEM TIME
© Susan Glendenning Art & Poetry

Totem Time

As the starry night bows *"Adieu"* To the good morning
songs of creatures great & small … I am blessed. As one
heron spreads his wings and glides in serene delight,
As campfires blaze in each one's heart … so do I
As Totem wolf howls his gratitude and Eagle people speak their truth
The All-Knowing answers me in every living thing…
…Now go forth, be the bliss that's you

CO-CREATING WITH THE DIVINE

E very time I close my eyes to look within for my Beloved Inner Being, I find a connecting sweetness that cleanses me of doubts and worries and holds me tight. Thank goodness I trusted enough to pray on that vision day thirty three years ago when I received my calling.

Respighi's music, *Ancient Aires and Dances* played softly on my stereo as I sat in bliss by the open window on the living room couch. I loved the combination of music and fir tree perfume. As I felt the utter bliss of the moment an alarming question overtook me. Life seemed destined to change so often… I loved my connection to Spirit. What if I lost my way, my connection to Spirit? Golden light glistened on the bark in the front yard. Surely it bespoke my Spirit? Such beauty always thrilled me. Of course I never wanted it to change.

Please, don't ever let go of me, I gasped. How will I keep my hand in yours? I implored. Then relaxing for an answer, I felt warmth and sweetness begin to fill me. Thank you for hearing me I began in my thoughts. Then, as I turned my eyes again to the window, the entire scene changed. The trees pulsed in psychedelic colors, sparkles of light intensified. Details of twig patterns and textures I had not seen seconds before, now appeared spectacularly clear. I could see with brilliant precision as if I just received my first pair of glasses. I saw a vibrant world overflowing with color, beauty and glistening life. Now as I crouched on my knees on the couch, face nearly pressed to the window in wonder, I heard these compelling words, *"Then express it in every medium I have given you."*

It took me some years to understand how my creative expressions with art, music, writing and a myriad other artistic endeavors, would secure my spiritual connection. Spirit's encouragement to trust myself and my Source however, was pivotal. It all seemed easy enough: continue to love nature and continue to look for and express my love of beauty in whatever form. The results of my trust were that creating has kept me resonating with appreciation, ever since. I enter the moment when I am creating and fully engage something primal and delicious in my heart. While painting, composing, writing, cooking, playing with my kids and friends, or by simply living full out… I get to play.

This trust became painfully clear right away in my art classes. If I dared to make a stroke that felt right but seemed odd, my art classes paid attention and also got bolder. We have all grown. Well, it worked. Every time I acted on my impulses, I would be rewarded. Being terrified before my classes felt strange! But that only prompted me to paint faster to stay ahead of my fears. That also worked. Then the most wonderful thing began… *Spirit began painting with me.*

Early in 2009, I painted a demo in front of a local art league. As I painted a pattern of hearts and birds, people in the audience began yelling out, "There's a fish. Oh my, there is another one!" Who knew what might appear next? It was all great fun and I got to play with the results. These paintings are delightful to look at, fun to explore and if you are lucky you might see a flying frog or a goddess in the garden! My students began to value authenticity and spontaneity. We all began to stay open looking for more inventions, for our own sense of beauty and learning. Especially for me, to see what surprises Spirit would bring. Oh, what adventures we get to live here, and so many filled with connection and growth. Spirit is VERY real. This I know.

Oh yes, Spirit also writes art poetry with me. And best of all, I get to help bring it forth! I start by simply describing whatever jumps out to me in the painting. Then my unseen helpers pop in with little surprise endings or phrases.

Many times I have laid my head on the piano keys and wept for the beauty of the melodies that come. Poetry and melody both float in from heaven and bring little O 'Henry revelations that explain everything and delight me. I love co-creating with my Spirit like this. I feel closer with every passing year. Spirit had a perfect plan for me, even when I did not completely understand the 'how's or why's' of it. "Have faith, soon enough you'll see the destination." whispered my Source.

Of course, I *can* trust myself with my Spirit. As I experience, grow and allow this connection I become more mindful of our presence together in the still moments and become more able to sense and respond from that inside-looking out-vantage. When I still myself to connect, let go of worries, and let myself realize what I really want... my whole outlook changes and when my outlook changes, my reality changes. Little by little I have come to know my true nature is love.

I am learning to trust this loving connection to sustain me, and to be with me, through me, as me always. Learning to trust myself and my Inner Being is what this part of my journey has been about. Spirit's loving encouragement to express and create ushers me into a world of positive connections that I can count on. So, don't be afraid. Engage your beloved Inner Being who loves to connect with you. I know It will lead us to all the joys we could ever want to unfurl.

Now I wonder what revelation we will discover next: *that we are all truly and eternally ONE big, beautiful, connected and creating being of love?* Well, just in case, I am holding on tight and ready for more.

THE DIVINE CIRCLE

Running...
bouncing lightly o'er the stones
floating like the Buddhist
who runs to find his OM

Rhythm of my heartbeat
filling spaces in my soul
fill them with your magic
till between them I can go

Running...
endless pathway of perceiving
where will my heart take me
I am following just being me

Distant among the clouds now
on steps to heaven rising high
in a mirror I see me coming
trailing glory through the sky

Running...
backward to the beginning
to my brothers and sisters
Oh..........I sigh

© Susan Flora

GLENDENNING

The Divine Circle was first published in 1995 by the National Library of Poetry in their book "The Sound of Poetry"

11419-10, Cronridge Drive PO Box 704, Owings Mills Maryland 21117

410-356-2000 (Susan's last name was Kyle in '1995)

As twinkling, dew-sparkled willow branches sway in love, go in peace,
care and with a heart full of helping… Love shall be your fill.
Susan

To order color prints of these fine art, pastel paintings,
please visit www.susanglendenning.com

Printed in the United States
by Baker & Taylor Publisher Services